John Keble

The First Edition of Keble's Christian Year

Being a facsimile of the editio princeps published in 1827. Vol. 2

John Keble

The First Edition of Keble's Christian Year
Being a facsimile of the editio princeps published in 1827. Vol. 2

ISBN/EAN: 9783337030247

Printed in Europe, USA, Canada, Australia, Japan

Cover: Foto ©Lupo / pixelio.de

More available books at **www.hansebooks.com**

THE CHRISTIAN YEAR.

THE

CHRISTIAN YEAR:

THOUGHTS IN VERSE

FOR THE

SUNDAYS AND HOLYDAYS

THROUGHOUT THE YEAR.

In quietness and in confidence shall be your strength.
Isaiah xxx. 15.

VOL. II

OXFORD,
PRINTED BY W. BAXTER,
FOR J. PARKER;
AND C. AND J. RIVINGTON, ST. PAUL'S CHURCH YARD,
AND WATERLOO PLACE, LONDON.
1827.

CONTENTS.

                                                                         Page

51. First Sunday after Trinity. Israel among the Ruins of Canaan.   1

52. Second Sunday after Trinity. Charity the Life of Faith.   4

53. Third Sunday after Trinity. Comfort for Sinners in the presence of the Good.   9

54. Fourth Sunday after Trinity. The Groans of Nature.   12

55. Fifth Sunday after Trinity. The Fishermen of Bethsaida.   18

56. Sixth Sunday after Trinity. The Psalmist repenting.   22

57. Seventh Sunday after Trinity. The Feast in the Wilderness.   26

58. Eighth Sunday after Trinity. The Disobedient Prophet.   30

59. Ninth Sunday after Trinity. Elijah in Horeb.   33

Contents.

60. Tenth Sunday after Trinity. Christ weeping over Jerusalem. 37
61. Eleventh Sunday after Trinity. Gehazi reproved. 40
62. Twelfth Sunday after Trinity. The Deaf and Dumb. 43
63. Thirteenth Sunday after Trinity. Moses on the Mount. 47
64. Fourteenth Sunday after Trinity. The Ten Lepers. 53
65. Fifteenth Sunday after Trinity. The Flowers of the Field. 56
66. Sixteenth Sunday after Trinity. Hope is better than Ease. 59
67. Seventeenth Sunday after Trinity. Ezekiel's Vision in the Temple. 62
68. Eighteenth Sunday after Trinity. The Church in the Wilderness. 66
69. Nineteenth Sunday after Trinity. Shadrach, Meshach, and Abednego. 71
70. Twentieth Sunday after Trinity. Mountain Scenery. 75
71. Twenty-first Sunday after Trinity. The Redbreast in September. 78
72. Twenty-second Sunday after Trinity. The Rule of Christian Forgiveness. 82

Contents.

73. Twenty-third Sunday after Trinity. Forest Leaves in Autumn. 85
74. Twenty-fourth Sunday after Trinity. Imperfection of Human Sympathy. 89
75. Twenty-fifth Sunday after Trinity. The Two Rainbows. 93
76. Last Sunday after Trinity. Self-examination before Advent. 97
77. St. Andrew's Day. 102
78. St. Thomas the Apostle. 105
79. Conversion of St. Paul. 110
80. Purification of St. Mary the Virgin. . . 115
81. St. Matthias' Day. 119
82. Annunciation of the Blessed Virgin Mary. 122
83. St. Mark's Day. 126
84. St. Philip and St. James's Day. ... 129
85. St. Barnabas the Apostle. 132
86. St. John Baptist's Day 136
87. St. Peter's Day. 140
88. St. James the Apostle. 144
89. St. Bartholomew the Apostle. . 147
90. St. Matthew the Apostle. ... 152
91. St. Michael and all Angels. 156
92. St. Luke the Evangelist. 161
93. St. Simon and St. Jude, Apostles. 166
94. All Saints' Day. 169

95. Holy Communion.	172
96. Holy Baptism.	177
97. Catechism.	180
98. Confirmation.	183
99. Matrimony.	186
100. Visitation and Communion of the Sick.	189
101. Burial of the Dead.	192
102. Churching of Women.	196
103. Commination.	198

LI.

FIRST SUNDAY AFTER TRINITY.

So Joshua smote all the country, and all their kings; he left none remaining. *Joshua* x. 40.

WHERE is the land with milk and honey flowing,
　The promise of our God, our fancy's theme?
Here over shatter'd walls dank weeds are growing,
　And blood and fire have run in mingled stream;
　　Like oaks and cedars all around
　　The giant corses strew the ground,
And haughty Jericho's cloud-piercing wall
Lies where it sank at Joshua's trumpet call.

These are not scenes for pastoral dance at even,
　For moonlight rovings in the fragrant glades,
Soft slumbers in the open eye of heaven,
　And all the listless joy of summer shades.

We in the midst of ruins live,
  Which every hour dread warning give,
Nor may our household vine or figtree hide
The broken arches of old Canaan's pride.

Where is the sweet repose of hearts repenting,
  The deep calm sky, the sunshine of the soul,
Now heaven and earth are to our bliss consenting,
  And all the Godhead joins to make us whole?
    The triple crown of mercy now
    Is ready for the suppliant's brow,
By the Almighty Three for ever plann'd,
And from behind the cloud held out by Jesus' hand.

"Now, Christians, hold your own—the land before ye
  "Is open—win your way, and take your rest."
So sounds our war-note; but our path of glory
  By many a cloud is darken'd and unblest:
    And daily as we downward glide,
    Life's ebbing stream on either side
Shews at each turn some mouldering hope or joy,
The Man seems following still the funeral of the Boy.

Open our eyes, thou Sun of life and gladness,
  That we may see that glorious world of thine!

First Sunday after Trinity.

It shines for us in vain, while drooping sadness
  Enfolds us here like mist: come pow'r benign,
    Touch our chill'd hearts with vernal smile,
    Our wintry course do Thou beguile,
Nor by the wayside ruins let us mourn,
Who have th' eternal towers for our appointed bourne.

LII.
SECOND SUNDAY AFTER TRINITY.

Marvel not, my brethren, if the world hate you. We know that we have passed from death unto life, because we love the brethren. 1 *St. John* iii. 13.

THE clouds that wrap the setting sun
   When Autumn's softest gleams are ending,
Where all bright hues together run
   In sweet confusion blending :—
Why, as we watch their floating wreath,
Seem they the breath of life to breathe?
To Fancy's eye their motions prove
They mantle round the Sun for love.

When up some woodland dale we catch
   The many twinkling smile[a] of ocean,

<blockquote>
[a] . . . . . . ποντίων τε κυμάτων
ἀνήριθμον γέλασμα. . . . .
Æschyl. Prom. 89.
</blockquote>

Or with pleas'd ear bewilder'd watch
   His chime of restless motion;
Still as the surging waves retire
They seem to gasp with strong desire,
Such signs of love old Ocean gives,
We cannot choose but think he lives.

Wouldst thou the life of souls discern?
   Nor human wisdom nor divine
Helps thee by aught beside to learn;
   Love is life's only sign.
The spring of the regenerate heart,
The pulse, the glow of every part,
Is the true love of Christ our Lord,
As man embrac'd, as God ador'd.

But he, whose heart will bound to mark
   The full bright burst of summer morn,
Loves too each little dewy spark
   By leaf or flow'ret worn:
Cheap forms, and common hues, 'tis true,
Through the bright shower-drop meet his view;
The colouring may be of this earth;
The lustre comes of heavenly birth.

Even so, who loves the Lord aright,
   No soul of man can worthless find ;
All will be precious in his sight,
   Since Christ on all hath shin'd :
But chiefly Christian souls ; for they,
Though worn and soil'd with sinful clay,
Are yet, to eyes that see them true,
All glistening with baptismal dew.

Then marvel not, if such as bask
   In purest light of innocence,
Hope against hope, in love's dear task,
   Spite of all dark offence.
If they who hate the trespass most,
Yet, when all other love is lost,
Love the poor sinner, marvel not,
Christ's mark outwears the rankest blot.

No distance breaks the tie of blood :
   Brothers are brothers evermore ;
Nor wrong, nor wrath of deadliest mood,
   That magic may o'erpower ;
Oft, ere the common source be known,
The kindred drops will claim their own,

Second Sunday after Trinity.

And throbbing pulses silently
Move heart towards heart by sympathy.

So is it with true Christian hearts;
   Their mutual share in Jesus' blood
An everlasting bond imparts
   Of holiest brotherhood:
Oh! might we all our lineage prove,
Give and forgive, do good and love,
By soft endearments in kind strife
Lightening the load of daily life!

There is much need: for not as yet
   Are we in shelter or repose,
The holy house is still beset
   With leaguer of stern foes;
Wild thoughts within, bad men without,
All evil spirits round about,
Are banded in unblest device,
To spoil Love's earthly paradise.

Then draw we nearer day by day,
   Each to his brethren, all to God;

Second Sunday after Trinity.

Let the world take us as she may,
   We must not change our road;
Not wondering, though in grief, to find
The martyr's foe still keep her mind;
But fix'd to hold Love's banner fast,
And by submission win at last.

LIII.
THIRD SUNDAY AFTER TRINITY.

There is joy in the presence of the angels of God over one sinner that repenteth. St. Luke xv. 10.

O HATEFUL spell of Sin! when friends are nigh,
   To make stern Memory tell her tale unsought,
And raise accusing shades of hours gone by,
   To come between us and all kindly thought!

Chill'd at her touch, the self-reproaching soul
   Flies from the heart and home she dearest loves
To where lone mountains tower, or billows roll,
   Or to your endless depth, ye solemn groves.

In vain: the averted cheek in loneliest dell
   Is conscious of a gaze it cannot bear,
The leaves that rustle near us seem to tell
   Our heart's sad secret to the silent air.

Nor is the dream untrue: for all around
    The heavens are watching with their thousand eyes,
We cannot pass our guardian angel's bound,
    Resign'd or sullen, he will hear our sighs.

He in the mazes of the budding wood
    Is near, and mourns to see our thankless glance
Dwell coldly, where the fresh green earth is strew'd
    With the first flowers that lead the vernal dance.

In wasteful bounty shower'd, they smile unseen,
    Unseen by man—but what if purer sprights
By moonlight o'er their dewy bosoms lean
    To' adore the Father of all gentle lights?

If such there be, O grief and shame to think
    That sight of thee should overcloud their joy,
A newborn soul, just waiting on the brink
    Of endless life, yet wrapt in earth's annoy!

O turn, and be thou turn'd! the selfish tear,
    In bitter thoughts of low born care begun,
Let it flow on, but flow refin'd and clear,
    The turbid waters brightening as they run.

Third Sunday after Trinity.

Let it flow on, till all thine earthly heart
    In penitential drops have ebb'd away,
Then fearless turn where Heaven hath set thy part,
    Nor shudder at the eye that saw thee stray.

O lost and found! all gentle souls below
    Their dearest welcome shall prepare, and prove
Such joy o'er thee, as raptur'd seraphs know,
    Who learn their lesson at the throne of love.

LIV.
FOURTH SUNDAY AFTER TRINITY.

> For the earnest expectation of the creature waiteth for the manifestations of the sons of God: for the creature was made subject to vanity, not willingly, but by reason of him who hath subjected the same in hope; because the creature itself also shall be delivered from the bondage of corruption into the glorious liberty of the children of God: for we know that the whole creation groaneth and travaileth in pain together until now. *Rom.* viii. 19.

It was not then a poet's dream,
 An idle vaunt of song,
Such as beneath the moon's soft gleam
 On vacant fancies throng;

Which bids us see in heaven and earth,
 In all fair things around,
Strong yearnings for a blest new birth
 With sinless glories crown'd;

Which bids us hear, at each sweet pause
    From care and want and toil,
When dewy eve her curtain draws
    Over the day's turmoil,

In the low chant of wakeful birds,
    In the deep weltering flood,
In whispering leaves, these solemn words—
    " God made us all for good."

All true, all faultless, all in tune,
    Creation's wondrous choir
Open'd in mystic unison
    To last till time expire.

And still it lasts : by day and night,
    With one consenting voice,
All hymn thy glory, Lord, aright,
    All worship and rejoice.

Man only mars the sweet accord,
    O'erpowering with "harsh din"
The music of thy works and word,
    Ill match'd with grief and sin.

Sin is with man at morning break,
    And through the live-long day
Deafens the ear that fain would wake
    To Nature's simple lay.

But when eve's silent foot-fall steals
    Along the eastern sky,
And one by one to earth reveals
    Those purer fires on high,

When one by one each human sound
    Dies on the awful ear,
Then Nature's voice no more is drown'd,
    She speaks and we must hear.

Then pours she on the Christian heart
    That warning still and deep,
At which high spirits of old would start
    Even from their Pagan sleep,

Just guessing, through their murky blind,
    Few, faint, and baffling sight,
Streaks of a brighter heaven behind,
    A cloudless depth of light.

Fourth Sunday after Trinity. 15

Such thoughts, the wreck of Paradise,
    Through many a dreary age,
Upbore whate'er of good and wise
    Yet lived in bard or sage :

They mark'd what agonizing throes
    Shook the great mother's womb;
But Reason's spells might not disclose
    The gracious birth to come ;

Nor could th' enchantress Hope forecast
    God's secret love and power;
The travail pangs of Earth must last
    Till her appointed hour ;

The hour that saw from opening heaven
    Redeeming glory stream,
Beyond the summer hues of even,
    Beyond the mid-day beam.

Thenceforth, to eyes of high desire,
    The meanest things below,
As with a seraph's robe of fire
    Invested, burn and glow:

The rod of heaven has touch'd them all,
 The word from heaven is spoken;
"Rise, shine, and sing, thou captive thrall;
 "Are not thy fetters broken?

"The God who hallow'd thee and blest,
 "Pronouncing thee all good—
"Hath He not all thy wrongs redrest,
 "And all thy bliss renew'd?

"Why mourn'st thou still as one bereft,
 "Now that th' eternal Son
"His blessed home in heaven hath left
 "To make thee all his own?"

Thou mourn'st because sin lingers still
 In Christ's new heaven and earth;
Because our rebel works and will
 Stain our immortal birth:

Because, as love and prayer grow cold,
 The Saviour hides his face,
And worldlings blot the temple's gold
 With uses vile and base.

Hence all thy groans and travail pains,
  Hence, till thy God return,
In wisdom's ear thy blithest strains,
  Oh Nature, seem to mourn.

LV.
FIFTH SUNDAY AFTER TRINITY.

And Simon answering said unto Him, Master, we have toiled all the night, and have taken nothing : nevertheless, at thy word I will let down the net : and when they had this done, they inclosed a great multitude of fishes, so that their net brake. *St. Luke* v. 5.

" THE livelong night we've toiled in vain,
    " But at thy gracious word
" I will let down the net again :—
    " Do thou thy will, O Lord!"

So spake the weary fisher, spent
    With bootless darkling toil,
Yet on his Master's bidding bent
    For love and not for spoil.

So day by day and week by week,
    In sad and weary thought,
They muse, whom God hath set to seek
    The souls his Christ hath bought.

Fifth Sunday after Trinity.

For not upon a tranquil lake
    Our pleasant task we ply,
Where all along our glistening wake
    The softest moonbeams lie;

Where rippling wave and dashing oar
    Our midnight chant attend,
Or whispering palm-leaves from the shore
    With midnight silence blend.

Sweet thoughts of peace, ye may not last:
    Too soon some ruder sound
Calls us from where ye soar so fast
    Back to our earthly round.

For wildest storms our ocean sweep:—
    No anchor but the cross
Might hold: and oft the thankless deep
    Turns all our toil to loss.

Full many a dreary anxious hour,
    We watch our nets alone
In drenching spray, and driving shower,
    And hear the night-bird's moan:

Fifth Sunday after Trinity.

At morn we look, and nought is there;
    Sad night brings cheerless day.
Who then from pining and despair
    The sickening heart can stay?

There is a stay—and we are strong;
    Our Master is at hand,
To cheer our solitary song,
    And guide us to the strand,

In his own time: but yet awhile
    Our bark at sea must ride;
Cast after cast, by force or guile
    All waters must be tried.

By blameless guile or gentle force,
    As when He deign'd to teach
(The load-star of our Christian course)
    Upon this sacred beach.

Should e'er thy wonder-working grace
    Triumph by our weak arm,
Let not our sinful fancy trac
    Aught human in the charm:

Fifth Sunday after Trinity. 21

To our own nets [b] ne'er bow we down,
    Lest on the eternal shore
The angels, while our draught they own [c],
    Reject us evermore:

Or, if for our unworthiness
    Toil, prayer, and watching fail,
In disappointment Thou canst bless,
    So love at heart prevail.

  [b] Habakkuk i. 16. They sacrifice unto their net, and burn incense unto their drag.
  [c] St. Matth. xiii. 49.

LVI.
SIXTH SUNDAY AFTER TRINITY.

David said unto Nathan, I have sinned against the Lord: and Nathan said unto David, The Lord also hath put away thy sin: thou shalt not die. 2 *Samuel* xii. 23.

 WHEN bitter thoughts, of conscience born,
   With sinners wake at morn,
 When from our restless couch we start,
 With fever'd lips and wither'd heart,
Where is the spell to charm those mists away,
And make new morning in that darksome day?
  One draught of spring's delicious air,
  One stedfast thought, that GOD is there.

 These are thy wonders, hourly wrought [d],
   Thou Lord of time and thought,
 Lifting and lowering souls at will,
 Crowding a world of good or ill

   [d] See Herbert's Poems, p. 160.

Sixth Sunday after Trinity.

Into a moment's vision: even as light
Mounts o'er a cloudy ridge, and all is bright,
   From west to east one thrilling ray
   Turning a wintry world to May.

Wouldst thou the pangs of guilt assuage?
     Lo here an open page,
   Where heavenly mercy shines as free,
   Written in balm, sad heart, for thee.
Never so fast, in silent April shower,
Flush'd into green the dry and leafless bower [e],
   As Israel's crowned mourner felt
   The dull hard stone within him melt.

The absolver saw the mighty grief,
     And hasten'd with relief;—
   "The Lord forgives; thou shalt not die:"—
   'Twas gently spoke, yet heard on high,
And all the band of angels, us'd to sing
In heaven, accordant to his raptur'd string,

---

[e] And all this leafless and uncolour'd scene
   Shall flush into variety again.
                    Cowper.

Who many a month had turn'd away
With veiled eyes, nor own'd his lay,

Now spread their wings, and throng around
    To the glad mournful sound,
And welcome, with bright open face,
The broken heart to love's embrace.
The rock is smitten, and to future years
Springs ever fresh the tide of holy tears [f]
    And holy music, whispering peace
    Till time and sin together cease.

There drink: and when ye are at rest,
    With that free Spirit blest [g],
Who to the contrite can dispense
The princely heart of innocence,
If ever, floating from faint earthly lyre,
Was wafted to your soul one high desire,
    By all the trembling hope ye feel,
    Think on the minstrel as ye kneel.

---

[f] Psalm li.

[g] Ps. li. 12. "Uphold me with thy *free* Spirit." The original word seems to mean "ingenuous, princely, noble." Read Bp. Horne's Paraphrase on the verse.

Sixth Sunday after Trinity.

Think on the shame, that dreadful hour
    When tears shall have no power,
Should his own lay th' accuser prove,
Cold while he kindled others' love.
And let your prayer for charity arise,
That his own heart may hear his melodies,
    And a true voice to him may cry,
"Thy God forgives—thou shalt not die.'

LVII.
SEVENTH SUNDAY AFTER TRINITY.

From whence can a man satisfy these men with bread here in the wilderness? *St. Mark* viii. 4.

GO not away, thou weary soul:
   Heaven has in store a precious dole
Even on Bethsaida's cold and darksome height,
   Where over rocks and sands arise
   Proud Sirion in the northern skies,
And Tabor's lonely peak, 'twixt thee and noon-day light.

   And far below, Gennesaret's main
   Spreads many a mile of liquid plain,
(Though all seem gather'd in one eager bound,)
   Then narrowing cleaves yon palmy lea,
   Towards that deep sulphureous sea,
Where five proud cities lie, by one dire sentence drown'd.

Seventh Sunday after Trinity.

Landscape of fear! yet, weary heart,
Thou needst not in thy gloom depart,
Nor fainting turn to seek thy distant home:
Sweetly thy sickening throbs are ey'd
By the kind Saviour at thy side;
For healing and for balm even now thine hour is come.

No fiery wing is seen to glide,
No cates ambrosial are supplied,
But one poor fisher's rude and scanty store
Is all He asks (and more than needs)
Who men and angels daily feeds,
And stills the wailing sea-bird on the hungry shore.

The feast is o'er, the guests are gone,
And over all that upland lone
The breeze of eve sweeps wildly as of old—
But far unlike the former dreams,
The heart's sweet moonlight softly gleams
Upon life's varied view, so joyless erst and cold.

As mountain travellers in the night,
When heaven by fits is dark and bright,

Pause listening on the silent heath, and hear
    Nor trampling hoof nor tinkling bell,
    Then bolder scale the rugged fell,
Conscious the more of One, ne'er seen, yet ever near :

    So when the tones of rapture gay
    On the lorn ear die quite away,
The lonely world seems lifted nearer heaven ;
    Seen daily, yet unmark'd before,
    Earth's common paths are strewn all o'er
With flowers of pensive hope, the wreath of man forgiven.

    The low sweet tones of Nature's lyre
    No more on listless ears expire,
Nor vainly smiles along the shady way
    The primrose in her vernal nest,
    Nor unlamented sink to rest
Sweet roses one by one, nor autumn leaves decay.

    There's not a star the heaven can shew,
    There's not a cottage hearth below,
But feeds with solace kind the willing soul—

Men love us, or they need our love;
Freely they own, or heedless prove
The curse of lawless hearts, the joy of self-control.

Then rouse thee from desponding sleep,
Nor by the wayside lingering weep,
Nor fear to seek Him farther in the wild,
Whose love can turn earth's worst and least
Into a conqueror's royal feast:
Thou wilt not be untrue, thou shalt not be beguil'd.

LVIII.
EIGHTH SUNDAY AFTER TRINITY.

It is the man of God, who was disobedient to the word of the Lord. 1 *Kings* xiii. 26.

Prophet of God, arise and take
With thee the words of wrath divine,
    The scourge of Heaven, to shake
    O'er yon apostate shrine.

Where angels down the lucid stair
Came hovering to our sainted sires,
    Now, in the twilight, glare
    The heathen's wizard fires.

Go, with thy voice the altar rend,
Scatter the ashes, be the arm,
    That idols would befriend,
    Shrunk at thy withering charm.

Eighth Sunday after Trinity.

Then turn thee, for thy time is short,
But trace not o'er the former way,
    Lest idol pleasures court
    Thy heedless soul astray.

Thou know'st how hard to hurry by,
Where on the lonely woodland road
    Beneath the moonlight sky
    The festal warblings flow'd;

Where maidens to the Queen of Heaven
Wove the gay dance round oak or palm,
    Or breath'd their vows at even
    In hymns as soft as balm.

Or thee perchance a darker spell
Enthralls: the smooth stones of the flood [h],
    By mountain grot or fell,
    Pollute with infants' blood;

The giant altar on the rock,
The cavern whence the timbrel's call

---

[h] *Isaiah* lvii. 6. Among the smooth stones of the stream is thy portion, they, they are thy lot.

Affrights the wandering flock:—
Thou long'st to search them all.

Trust not the dangerous path again—
O forward step and lingering will!
  O lov'd and warn'd in vain!
  And wilt thou perish still?

Thy message given, thine home in sight,
To the forbidden feast return?
  Yield to the false delight
  Thy better soul could spurn?

Alas, my brother! round thy tomb
In sorrow kneeling, and in fear,
  We read the Pastor's doom
  Who speaks and will not hear.

The grey-hair'd saint may fail at last
The surest guide a wanderer prove
  Death only binds us fast
  To the bright shore of love.

LIX.
NINTH SUNDAY AFTER TRINITY.

And after the earthquake a fire; but the Lord was not in the fire: and after the fire, a still small voice. 1 *Kings* xix. 12.

IN troublous days of anguish and rebuke,
While sadly round them Israel's children look,
    And their eyes fail for waiting on their Lord:
While underneath each awful arch of green,
On every mountain top, God's chosen scene
    Of pure heart-worship, Baal is ador'd:

'Tis well, true hearts should for a time retire
To holy ground, in quiet to aspire
    Towards promis'd regions of serener grace;
On Horeb, with Elijah, let us lie,
Where all around on mountain, sand, and sky,
    God's chariot-wheels have left distinctest trace:

There, if in jealousy and strong disdain
We to the sinner's God of sin complain,
 Untimely seeking here the peace of heaven—
"It is enough, O Lord! now let me die
"Even as my fathers did: for what am I
 "That I should stand, where they have vainly
  "striven?"—

Perhaps our God may of our conscience ask,
"What doest thou here, frail wanderer from thy task?
 "Where hast thou left those few sheep in the wild [a]?"
Then should we plead our heart's consuming pain,
At sight of ruin'd altars, prophets slain,
 And God's own ark with blood of souls defil'd;

He on the rock may bid us stand, and see
The outskirts of his march of mystery,
 His endless warfare with man's wilful heart;
First, His great Power He to the sinner shews,
Lo! at His angry blast the rocks unclose,
 And to their base the trembling mountains part:

Yet the Lord is not here: 'tis not by Power
He will be known—but darker tempests lower;

  [a] 1 Sam. xvii. 28.

Ninth Sunday after Trinity.

Still, sullen heavings vex the labouring ground:
Perhaps His Presence thro' all depth and height,
Best of all gems, that deck his crown of light,
   The haughty eye may dazzle and confound.

God is not in the earthquake; but behold
From Sinai's caves are bursting, as of old,
   The flames of His consuming jealous ire.
Woe to the sinner, should stern Justice prove
His chosen attribute;—but He in love
   Hastes to proclaim, "God is not in the fire."

The storm is o'er—and hark! a still small voice
Steals on the ear, to say, Jehovah's choice
   Is ever with the soft, meek, tender soul:
By soft, meek, tender ways He loves to draw
The sinner, startled by his ways of awe:
   Here is our Lord, and not where thunders roll.

Back then, complainer; loath thy life no more,
Nor deem thyself upon a desert shore,
   Because the rocks the nearer prospect close.
Yet in fallen Israel are there hearts and eyes
That day by day in prayer like thine arise:
   Thou know'st them not, but their Creator knows.

Go, to the world return, nor fear to cast
Thy bread upon the waters, sure at last [b]
    In joy to find it after many days.
The work be thine, the fruit thy children's part :
Choose to believe, not see : sight tempts the heart
    From sober walking in true Gospel ways.

[b] Eccles. xi. 1.

LX.

TENTH SUNDAY AFTER TRINITY.

And when he was come near, he beheld the city, and wept over it. *St. Luke* xix. 41.

WHY doth my Saviour weep
 At sight of Sion's bowers?
Shows it not fair from yonder steep,
 Her gorgeous crown of towers?
Mark well his holy pains:
 'Tis not in pride or scorn,
That Israel's King with sorrow stains
 His own triumphal morn.

It is not that his soul
 Is wandering sadly on,
In thought how soon at death's dark goal
 Their course will all be run,
Who now are shouting round
 Hosanna to their chief;

No thought like this in Him is found,
    This were a Conqueror's grief.

Or doth he feel the cross
    Already in his heart,
The pain, the shame, the scorn, the loss?
    Feel even his God depart?
No: though he knew full well
    The grief that then shall be—
The grief that angels cannot tell—
    Our God in agony.

It is not thus he mourns;
    Such might be Martyr's tears,
When his last lingering look he turns
    On human hopes and fears;
But hero ne'er or saint
    The secret load might know,
With which His spirit waxeth faint;
    His is a Saviour's woe.

" If thou hadst known, even thou,
    " At least in this thy day,
" The message of thy peace! but now
    " 'Tis pass'd for aye away:

"Now foes shall trench thee round,
　"And lay thee even with earth,
"And dash thy children to the ground,
　"Thy glory and thy mirth."

And doth the Saviour weep
　Over his people's sin,
Because we will not let him keep
　The souls He died to win?
Ye hearts, that love the Lord,
　If at this sight ye burn,
See that in thought, in deed, in word,
　Ye hate what made Him mourn.

LXI.

ELEVENTH SUNDAY AFTER TRINITY.

Is it a time to receive money, and to receive garments, and olive yards, and vineyards, and sheep, and oxen, and men servants, and maid servants? 2 *Kings* v. 26.

IS this a time to plant and build,
Add house to house, and field to field,
When round our walls the battle lowers,
When mines are sprung beneath our towers,
And watchful foes are stealing round
To search and spoil the holy ground?

Is this a time for moonlight dreams
Of love and home by mazy streams,
For Fancy with her shadowy toys,
Aerial hopes and pensive joys,
While souls are wandering far and wide,
And curses swarm on every side?

No—rather steel thy melting heart
To act the martyr's sternest part,
To watch, with firm unshrinking eye,
Thy darling visions as they die,
Till all bright hopes, and hues of day
Have faded into twilight gray.

Yes—let them pass without a sigh,
And if the world seem dull and dry,
If long and sad thy lonely hours,
And winds have rent thy sheltering bowers,
Bethink thee what thou art and where,
A sinner in a life of care.

The fire of Heaven is soon to fall,
(Thou know'st it) on this earthly ball;
Then many a soul, the price of blood,
Mark'd by th' Almighty's hand for good,
Shall feel the o'erflowing whirlwinds sweep—
And will the blessed Angels weep?

Then in his wrath shall GOD uproot
The trees He set, for lack of fruit,
And drown in rude tempestuous blaze
The towers His hand had deign'd to raise;

In silence, ere that storm begin,
Count o'er His mercies and thy sin.

Pray only that thine aching heart,
From visions vain content to part,
Strong for Love's sake its woe to hide,
May cheerful wait the cross beside,
Too happy if, that dreadful day,
Thy life be given thee for a prey [c].

Snatch'd sudden from th' avenging rod,
Safe in the bosom of thy GOD,
How wilt thou then look back, and smile
On thoughts that bitterest seem'd erewhile,
And bless the pangs that made thee see,
This was no world of rest for thee.

[c] *Jeremiah* xlv. 4, 5. The Lord saith thus: Behold, that which I have built will I break down, and that which I have planted I will pluck up, even this whole land. And seekest thou great things for thyself? seek them not, for, behold, I will bring evil upon all flesh, saith the Lord; but thy life will I give unto thee for a prey in all places whither thou goest.

LXII.
TWELFTH SUNDAY AFTER TRINITY.

And looking up to Heaven, He sighed, and saith unto him, Ephphatha, that is, Be opened. *Mark* vii. 34.

THE Son of God in doing good
    Was fain to look to heaven and sigh :
And shall the heirs of sinful blood
    Seek joy unmix'd in charity ?
God will not let Love's work impart
Full solace, lest it steal the heart;
Be thou content in tears to sow,
Blessing, like Jesus, in thy woe.

He look'd to heaven, and sadly sigh'd—
    What saw my gracious Saviour there,
With fear and anguish to divide
    The joy of Heaven-accepted prayer ?

So o'er the bed where Lazarus slept
He to his Father groan'd and wept :
What saw he mournful in that grave,
Knowing himself so strong to save ?

O'erwhelming thoughts of pain and grief
   Over his sinking spirit sweep ;—
" What boots it gathering one lost leaf
  " Out of yon sere and wither'd heap,
" Where souls and bodies, hopes and joys,
" All that earth owns or sin destroys,
" Under the spurning hoof are cast,
" Or tossing in th' autumnal blast?"

The deaf may hear the Saviour's voice,
   The fetter'd tongue its chain may break ;
But the deaf heart, the dumb by choice,
   The laggard soul, that will not wake,
The guilt that scorns to be forgiven ;—
These baffle e'en the spells of heaven ;
In thought of these, his brows benign
Not even in healing cloudless shine.

No eye but His might ever bear
   To gaze all down that drear abyss,

Twelfth Sunday after Trinity.

Because none ever saw so clear
   The shore beyond of endless bliss :
The giddy waves so restless hurl'd,
The vex'd pulse of this feverish world,
He views and counts with steady sight,
Used to behold the Infinite.

But that in such communion high
   He hath a fount of strength within,
Sure His meek heart would break and die,
   O'erburthen'd by his brethren's sin ;
Weak eyes on darkness dare not gaze,
It dazzles like the noon-day blaze ;
But he who sees God's face may brook
On the true face of Sin to look.

What then shall wretched sinners do,
   When in their last, their hopeless day,
Sin, as it is, shall meet their view,
   God turn his face for aye away?
Lord, by thy sad and earnest eye,
When Thou didst look to heaven and sigh;
Thy voice, that with a word could chase
The dumb, deaf spirit from his place ;

As thou hast touch'd our ears, and taught
    Our tongues to speak thy praises plain,
Quell thou each thankless godless thought
    That would make fast our bonds again.
From wordly strife, from mirth unblest,
Drowning thy music in the breast,
From foul reproach, from thrilling fears,
Preserve, good Lord, thy servants' ears.

From idle words, that restless throng,
    And haunt our hearts when we would pray,
From pride's false chime, and jarring wrong,
    Seal thou my lips, and guard the way:
For Thou hast sworn, that every ear,
Willing or loth, thy trump shall hear,
And every tongue unchained be
To own no hope, no God, but Thee.

LXIII.
THIRTEENTH SUNDAY AFTER TRINITY.

And he turned him unto his disciples, and said privately, Blessed are the eyes which see the things that ye see: for I tell you, that many prophets and kings have desired to see those things which ye see, and have not seen them; and to hear those things which ye hear, and have not heard them. *St. Luke* x. 23, 24.

ON Sinai's top, in prayer and trance,
   Full forty nights and forty days
The Prophet watch'd for one dear glance
   Of Thee and of thy ways:

Fasting he watch'd and all alone,
   Wrapt in a still, dark, solid cloud,
The curtain of the Holy One
   Drawn round him like a shroud:

So, separate from the world, his breast
    Might duly take and strongly keep
The print of Heaven, to be express'd
    Ere long on Sion's steep [i].

There one by one his spirit saw,
    Of things divine the shadows bright,
The pageant of God's perfect law;
    Yet felt not full delight.

Through gold and gems, a dazzling maze,
    From veil to veil the vision led,
And ended, where unearthly rays
    From o'er the Ark were shed.

Yet not that gorgeous place, nor aught
    Of human or angelic frame,
Could half appease his craving thought;
    The void was still the same.

" Shew me thy glory, gracious Lord!
    " 'Tis Thee," he cries, "not thine, I seek [k]."—

---

[i] See that thou make all things according to the pattern shewed to thee in the mount. *Hebrews* viii. 5.

[k] Exodus xxxiii. 18.

Thirteenth Sunday after Trinity.

Nay, start not at so bold a word
   From man, frail worm and weak:

The spark of his first deathless fire
   Yet buoys him up, and high above
The holiest creature, dares aspire
   To the Creator's love.

The eye in smiles may wander round,
   Caught by earth's shadows as they fleet;
But for the soul no help is found,
   Save Him, who made it, meet.

Spite of yourselves, ye witness this [k],
   Who blindly self or sense adore;
Else wherefore leaving your own bliss
   Still restless ask ye more?

This witness bore the saints of old
   When highest rapt and favour'd most,
Still seeking precious things untold,
   Not in fruition lost.

      [k] Pensees de Pascal, part 1. art. viii.

Canaan was theirs, and in it all
  The proudest hope of kings dare claim ;
Sion was theirs ; and at their call
  Fire from Jehovah came.

Yet monarchs walk'd as pilgrims still
  In their own land, earth's pride and grace ;
And seers would mourn on Sion's hill
  Their Lord's averted face.

Vainly they tried the deeps to sound
  Even of their own prophetic thought,
When of Christ crucified and crown'd
  His Spirit in them taught :

But He their aching gaze repress'd
  Which sought behind the veil to see,
For not without us fully bless'd [1]
  Or perfect might they be.

The rays of the Almighty's face
  No sinner's eye might then receive ;

---

[1] Hebrews xl. 40. That they without us should not be made perfect.

Thirteenth Sunday after Trinity. 51

Only the meekest man found grace [m]
    To see his skirts and live.

But we as in a glass espy
    The glory of His countenance,
Not in a whirlwind hurrying by
    The too presumptuous glance,

But with mild radiance every hour
    From our dear Saviour's face benign
Bent on us with transforming power,
    Till we, too, faintly shine.

Sprinkled with his atoning blood
    Safely before our God we stand,
As on the rock the Prophet stood,
    Beneath His shadowing hand.—

Bless'd eyes, which see the things we see!
    And yet this tree of life hath prov'd
To many a soul a poison tree,
    Beheld, and not belov'd.

        [m] Exod. xxxiii. 20...23.

So like an angel's is our bliss
    (Oh! thought to comfort and appall)
It needs must bring, if us'd amiss,
    An angel's hopeless fall.

LXIV.
FOURTEENTH SUNDAY AFTER TRINITY.

And Jesus answering said, Were there not ten cleansed? but where are the nine? There are not found that returned to give glory to God, save this stranger. St. Luke xvii. 17, 18.

TEN cleans'd, and only one remain!
Who would have thought our nature's stain
Was dyed so foul, so deep in grain?
 Even He who reads the heart,—
Knows what He gave and what we lost,
Sin's forfeit, and redemption's cost,—
By a short pang of wonder cross'd
 Seems at the sight to start:

Yet 'twas not wonder, but His love
Our wavering spirits would reprove,
That heaven-ward seem so free to move
 When earth can yield no more:

Then from afar on God we cry;
But should the mist of woe roll by,
Not showers across an April sky
    Drift, when the storm is o'er

Faster than those false drops and few
Fleet from the heart, a worthless dew.
What sadder scene can angels view
    Than self-deceiving tears,
Pour'd idly over some dark page
Of earlier life, while pride or rage
The record of to-day engage,
    A woe for future years?

Spirits, that round the sick man's bed
Watch'd, noting down each prayer he made,
Were your unerring roll display'd,
    His pride of health to' abase;
Or, when soft showers in season fall
Answering a famish'd nation's call,
Should unseen fingers on the wall
    Our vows forgotten trace;

How should we gaze in trance of fear!
Yet shines the light as thrilling clear

From heaven upon that scroll severe,
    " Ten cleans'd and one remain !"
Nor surer would the blessing prove
Of humbled hearts, that own thy love,
Should choral welcomes from above
    Visit our senses plain :

Than by Thy placid voice and brow,
With healing first, with comfort now,
Turn'd upon him, who hastes to bow
    Before thee, heart and knee ;
" Oh ! thou, who only would'st be blest,
" On thee alone my blessing rest !
" Rise, go thy way, in peace, possess'd
    " For evermore of me."

LXV.
FIFTEENTH SUNDAY AFTER TRINITY.

Consider the lilies of the field, how they grow.   *St. Matt.* vi. 28.

SWEET nurslings of the vernal skies,
   Bath'd in soft airs, and fed with dew,
What more than magic in you lies,
   To fill the heart's fond view?
In childhood's sports, companions gay,
In sorrow, on Life's downward way,
How soothing! in our last decay
   Memorials prompt and true.

Relics ye are of Eden's bowers,
   As pure, as fragrant, and as fair,
As when ye crown'd the sunshine hours
   Of happy wanderers there.

Fifteenth Sunday after Trinity.

Fall'n all beside—the world of life,
How is it stain'd with fear and strife!
In Reason's world what storms are rife,
   What passions range and glare!

But cheerful and unchang'd the while
   Your first and perfect form ye shew,
The same that won Eve's matron smile
   In the world's opening glow.
The stars of Heaven a course are taught
Too high above our human thought;—
Ye may be found if ye are sought,
   And as we gaze, we know.

Ye dwell beside our paths and homes,
   Our paths of sin, our homes of sorrow,
And guilty man, where'er he roams,
   Your innocent mirth may borrow.
The birds of air before us fleet,
They cannot brook our shame to meet—
But we may taste your solace sweet
   And come again to-morrow.

Ye fearless in your nests abide—
   Nor may we scorn, too proudly wise,

Your silent lessons, undescried
  By all but lowly eyes:
For ye could draw th' admiring gaze
Of Him who worlds and hearts surveys:
Your order wild, your fragrant maze,
  He taught us how to prize.

Ye felt your Maker's smile that hour,
  As when He paus'd and own'd you good;
His blessing on earth's primal bower,
  Ye felt it all renew'd.
What care ye now, if winter's storm
Sweep ruthless o'er each silken form?
Christ's blessing at your heart is warm,
  Ye fear no vexing mood.

Alas! of thousand bosoms kind,
  That daily court you and caress,
How few the happy secret find
  Of your calm loveliness!
" Live for to-day! to-morrow's light
" To-morrow's cares shall bring to sight.
" Go sleep like closing flowers at night,
  " And Heaven thy morn will bless."

LXVI.
SIXTEENTH SUNDAY AFTER TRINITY.

I desire that ye faint not at my tribulations for you, which is your glory. Ephesians *iii. 13.*

WISH not, dear friends, my pain away—
   Wish me a wise and thankful heart,
With GOD, in all my griefs, to stay,
   Nor from His lov'd correction start.

The dearest offering He can crave
   His portion in our souls to prove,
What is it to the gift He gave,
   The only Son of His dear love?

But we, like vex'd unquiet sprights,
   Will still be hovering o'er the tomb,
Where buried lie our vain delights,
   Nor sweetly take a sinner's doom.

Sixteenth Sunday after Trinity.

In Life's long sickness evermore
   Our thoughts are tossing to and fro:
We change our posture o'er and o'er,
   But cannot rest, nor cheat our woe.

Were it not better to lie still,
   Let Him strike home and bless the rod,
Never so safe as when our will
   Yields undiscern'd by all but God?

Thy precious things, whate'er they be
   That haunt and vex thee, heart and brain,
Look to the Cross, and thou shalt see
   How thou may'st turn them all to gain.

Lovest thou praise? the Cross is shame:
   Or ease? the Cross is bitter grief:
More pangs than tongue or heart can frame
   Were suffer'd there without relief.

We of that altar would partake,
   But cannot quit the cost—no throne
Is ours, to leave for Thy dear sake—
   We cannot do as Thou hast done.

Sixteenth Sunday after Trinity.

We cannot part with Heaven for Thee—
   Yet guide us in thy track of love:
Let us gaze on where light should be,
   Though not a beam the clouds remove.

So wanderers ever fond and true
   Look homeward through the evening sky,
Without a streak of heaven's soft blue
   To aid Affection's dreaming eye.

The wanderer seeks his native bower,
   And we will look and long for Thee,
And thank thee for each trying hour,
   Wishing, not struggling, to be free.

LXVII.
SEVENTEENTH SUNDAY AFTER TRINITY.

Every man of the house of Israel that setteth up his idols in his heart, and putteth the stumbling-block of his iniquity before his face, and cometh to the Prophet, I the Lord will answer him according to the multitude of his idols. *Ezeiel* xiv. 4.

STATELY thy walls, and holy are the prayers,
   Which day and night before thine altars rise ;
Not statelier, towering o'er her marble stairs,
   Flash'd Sion's gilded dome to summer skies,
Not holier, while around him angels bow'd,
From Aaron's censer steam'd the spicy cloud,

Before the mercy-seat. O mother dear,
   Wilt thou forgive thy son one boding sigh ?
Forgive, if round thy towers he walk in fear,
   And tell thy jewels o'er with jealous eye ?

Seventeenth Sunday after Trinity.

Mindful of that sad vision, which in thought ᵐ
From Chebar's plains the captive prophet brought

To see lost Sion's shame. 'Twas morning prime,
　And like a Queen new seated on her throne,
God's crowned mountain, as in happier time,
　Seem'd to rejoice in sunshine all her own;
So bright, while all in shade around her lay,
Her northern pinnacles had caught th' emerging ray.

The dazzling lines of her majestic roof
　Cross'd with as free a span the vault of Heaven,
As when twelve tribes knelt silently aloof,
　Ere God his answer to their king had given ⁿ,
Ere yet upon the new-built altar fell
The glory of the Lord, the Lord of Israel.

All seems the same: but enter in and see
　What idol shapes are on the wall pourtray'd ᵒ:
And watch their shameless and unholy glee,
　Who worship there in Aaron's robes array'd:
Hear Judah's maids the dirge to Thammuz pour ᵖ,
And mark her chiefs yon orient sun adore ᑫ.

ᵐ Ezekiel viii. 3.　　ⁿ 1 Kings viii. 5.　　ᵒ Ezekiel viii. 10.
ᵖ Ezekiel viii. 14.　　ᑫ Ezekiel viii. 16.

Yet turn thee, Son of man—for worse than these
    Thou must behold: thy loathing were but lost
On dead men's crimes, and Jews' idolatries—
    Come learn to tell aright thine own sins' cost,—
And sure their sin as far from equals thine,
As earthly hopes abus'd are less than hopes divine.

What if within His world, His church, our LORD
    Have enter'd thee, as in some temple gate,
Where, looking round, each glance might thee afford
    Some glorious earnest of thine high estate,
And thou, false heart and frail, hast turn'd from all
To worship pleasure's shadow on the wall.

If, when the LORD of Glory was in sight,
    Thou turn thy back upon that fountain clear,
To bow before the "little drop of light,"
    Which dim-eyed men call praise and glory here;
What dost thou, but adore the sun, and scorn
Him at whose only word both sun and stars were born?

If, while around thee gales from Eden breathe,
    Thou hide thine eyes, to make thy peevish moan
Over some broken reed of earth beneath,
    Some darling of blind fancy dead and gone,

Seventeenth Sunday after Trinity.

As wisely might'st thou in JEHOVAH's fane
Offer thy love and tears to Thammuz slain.

Turn thee from these, or dare not to enquire
   Of Him whose name is Jealous, lest in wrath
He hear and answer thine unblest desire:
   Far better we should cross his lightning's path
Than be according to our idols heard,
And GOD should take us at our own vain word.

Thou, who hast deign'd the Christian's heart to call
Thy Church and Shrine; whene'er our rebel will
Would in that chosen home of thine instal
   Belial or Mammon, grant us not the ill
We blindly ask; in very love refuse
Whate'er thou know'st our weakness would abuse.

Or rather help us, LORD, to choose the good,
   To pray for nought, to seek to none, but Thee,
Nor by "our daily bread" mean common food,
   Nor say, "From this world's evil set us free;"
Teach us to love, with CHRIST, our sole true bliss,
Else, though in CHRIST's own words, we surely pray
   amiss.

LXVIII.
EIGHTEENTH SUNDAY AFTER TRINITY.

I will bring you into the wilderness of the people, and there will I plead with you face to face: like as I pleaded with your fathers in the wilderness of the land of Egypt, so will I plead with you, saith the Lord God.   *Ezekiel* xx. 35, 36.

IT is so—ope thine eyes, and see—
   What view'st thou all around?
A desert, where iniquity
   And knowledge both abound.

In the waste howling wilderness
   The Church is wandering still [a],
Because we would not onward press
   When close to Sion's hill.

Back to the world we faithless turn'd,
   And far along the wild,

[a] Revelations xiii. 14.

Eighteenth Sunday after Trinity.

With labour lost and sorrow earn'd,
   Our steps have been beguil'd.

Yet full before us, all the while,
   The shadowing pillar stays,
The living waters brightly smile,
   Th' eternal turrets blaze.

Yet Heaven is raining angels' bread
   To be our daily food,
And fresh, as when it first was shed,
   Springs forth the SAVIOUR's blood.

From every region, race, and speech,
   Believing myriads throng,
Till, far as sin and sorrow reach,
   Thy grace is spread along.

Till sweetest nature, brightest art,
   Their votive incense bring,
And every voice and every heart
   Own Thee their God and King.

All own; but few, alas! will love;
   Too like the recreant band

That with thy patient Spirit strove
    Upon the Red-sea strand.

O Father of long-suffering grace,
    Thou who hast sworn to stay
Pleading with sinners face to face
    Through all their devious way,

How shall we speak to Thee, O LORD,
    Or how in silence lie?
Look on us, and we are abhorr'd,
    Turn from us, and we die.

Thy guardian fire, thy guiding cloud,
    Still let them gild our wall,
Nor be our foes and thine allow'd
    To see us faint and fall.

Too oft, within this camp of thine,
    Rebellious murmurs rise;
Sin cannot bear to see thee shine
    So awful to her eyes.

Fain would our lawless hearts escape,
    And with the heathen be,

Eighteenth Sunday after Trinity.

To worship every monstrous shape
    In fancied darkness free [b].

Vain thought, that shall not be at all!
    Refuse we or obey,
Our ears have heard th' Almighty's call,
    We cannot be as they.

We cannot hope the heathen's doom,
    To whom GOD's Son is given,
Whose eyes have seen beyond the tomb,
    Who have the key of Heaven.

Weak tremblers on the edge of woe,
    Yet shrinking from true bliss,
Our rest must be " no rest below,"
    And let our prayer be this:

" LORD, wave again thy chastening rod,
    " Till every idol throne
" Crumble to dust, and Thou, O GOD,
    " Reign in our hearts alone.

---

[b] Ezekiel xx. 32. That which cometh into your mind shall not be at all, that ye say, We will be as the heathen, as the families of the countries, to serve wood and stone.

Eighteenth Sunday after Trinity.

"Bring all our wandering fancies home,
  "For Thou hast every spell,
"And 'mid the heathen where they roam,
  "Thou knowest, LORD, too well.

"Thou know'st our service sad and hard,
  "Thou know'st us fond and frail;—
"Win us to be belov'd and spar'd
  "When all the world shall fail.

"So when at last our weary days
  "Are well-nigh wasted here,
"And we can trace thy wondrous ways
  "In distance calm and clear,

"When in thy love and Israel's sin
  "We read our story true,
"We may not, all too late, begin
  "To wish our hopes were new :

"Long lov'd, long tried, long spar'd as they,
  "Unlike in this alone,
"That, by thy grace, our hearts shall stay
  "For evermore thine own."

LXIX.
NINETEENTH SUNDAY AFTER TRINITY.

Then Nebuchadnezzar the King was astonied, and rose up in haste, and spake, and said unto his counsellors, Did not we cast three men bound into the midst of the fire? They answered and said unto the King, True, O King. He answered and said, Lo, I see four men loose, walking in the midst of the fire, and they have no hurt; and the form of the fourth is like the Son of God. *Daniel* iii. 25.

WHEN Persecution's torrent blaze
    Wraps the unshrinking Martyr's head;
When fade all earthly flowers and bays,
    When summer friends are gone and fled,
Is he alone in that dark hour,
Who owns the Lord of love and power?

Or waves there not around his brow
    A wand no human arm may wield,
Fraught with a spell no angels know,
    His steps to guide, his soul to shield?

Nineteenth Sunday after Trinity.

Thou, Saviour, art his charmed bower,
His magic ring, his rock, his tower.

And when the wicked ones behold
   Thy favourites walking in thy light,
Just as, in fancied triumph bold
   They deem'd them lost in deadly night,
Amaz'd they cry, " What spell is this,
" Which turns their sufferings all to bliss ?

" How are they free whom we had bound,
   " Upright, whom in the gulf we cast ?
" What wondrous helper have they found
   " To screen them from the scorching blast?
" Three were they—who hath made them four ?
" And sure a form divine he wore,

" Even like the Son of God." So cried
   The Tyrant, when in one fierce flame
The martyrs liv'd, the murderers died :
   Yet knew he not what angel came
To make the rushing fire-flood seem
Like summer breeze by woodland stream [b].

---

[b] Song of the Three Children, ver. 27. " As it had been a moist whistling wind."

He knew not, but there are who know:
   The Matron, who alone has stood,
When not a prop seem'd left below,
   The first torn hour of widowhood,
Yet cheer'd and cheering all, the while,
With sad but unaffected smile;—

The Father, who his vigil keeps
   By the sad couch whence hope has flown,
Watching the eye where reason sleeps,
   Yet in his heart can mercy own,
Still sweetly yielding to the rod,
Still loving man, still thanking GOD;—

The Christian Pastor, bow'd to earth
   With thankless toil, and vile esteem'd,
Still travailing in second birth
   Of souls that will not be redeem'd,
Yet stedfast set to do his part,
And fearing most his own vain heart;—

These know: on these look long and well,
   Cleansing thy sight by prayer and faith,

And thou shalt know what secret spell
Preserves them in their living death :
Though sevenfold flames thine eye shall see
The Saviour walking with his faithful Three.

LX.
TWENTIETH SUNDAY AFTER TRINITY.

Hear, O ye mountains, the Lord's controversy, and ye strong foundations of the earth. *Micah* vi. 7.

WHERE is thy favour'd haunt, eternal Voice,
    The region of thy choice,
Where, undisturb'd by sin and earth, the soul
    Owns thine entire control?—
'Tis on the mountain's summit dark and high,
    When storms are hurrying by:
'Tis 'mid the strong foundations of the earth,
    Where torrents have their birth.

No sounds of worldly toil, ascending there,
    Mar the full burst of prayer;
Lone Nature feels that she may freely breathe,
    And round us and beneath

Are heard her sacred tones: the fitful sweep
    Of winds across the steep,
Through wither'd bents—romantic note and clear,
    Meet for a hermit's ear,—

The wheeling kite's wild solitary cry,
    And, scarcely heard so high,
The dashing waters when the air is still
    From many a torrent rill
That winds unseen beneath the shaggy fell,
    Track'd by the blue mist well:
Such sounds as make deep silence in the heart
    For Thought to do her part.

'Tis then we hear the voice of God within,
    Pleading with care and sin:
"Child of my love! how have I wearied thee?
    " Why wilt thou err from me?
" Have I not brought thee from the house of slaves,
    " Parted the drowning waves,
" And set my saints before thee in the way,
    " Lest thou should faint or stray?

" What? was the promise made to thee alone?
    " Art thou th' excepted one?

Twentieth Sunday after Trinity.

"An heir of glory without grief or pain?
 "O vision false and vain!
"There lies thy cross; beneath it meekly bow;
 "It fits thy stature now:
"Who scornful pass it with averted eye,
 "'Twill crush them by and by.

"Raise thy repining eyes, and take true measure
 "Of thine eternal treasure;
"The Father of thy Lord can grudge thee nought,
 "The world for thee was bought,
"And as this landscape broad—earth, sea, and sky,—
 "All centers in thine eye,
"So all God does, if rightly understood,
 "Shall work thy final good."

LXXI.
TWENTY-FIRST SUNDAY AFTER TRINITY.

The vision is yet for an appointed time ; but at the end it shall speak and not lie: though it tarry, wait for it, because it will surely come, it will not tarry. *Habakkuk* ii. 3.

THE morning mist is clear'd away,
  Yet still the face of heaven is grey,
Nor yet th' autumnal breeze has stirr'd the grove,
  Faded yet full, a paler green
  Skirts soberly the tranquil scene,
The red-breast warbles round this leafy cove.

  Sweet messenger of "calm decay,"
  Saluting sorrow as you may,
As one still bent to find or make the best,

In thee, and in this quiet mead
The lesson of sweet peace I read,
Rather in all to be resign'd than blest.

'Tis a low chant, according well
With the soft solitary knell,
As homeward from some grave belov'd we turn,
Or by some holy death-bed dear,
Most welcome to the chasten'd ear
Of her whom heaven is teaching how to mourn.

O cheerful tender strain! the heart
That duly bears with you its part,
Singing so thankful to the dreary blast,
Though gone and spent its joyous prime,
And on the world's autumnal time,
'Mid wither'd hues and sere, its lot be cast.

That is the heart for thoughtful seer,
Watching, in trance nor dark nor clear ^d,

---

^d Zechariah xiv. 6. It shall come to pass in that day, that the night shall not be clear nor dark.

Th' o'erwhelming future as it nearer draws :
   His spirit calm'd the storm to meet,
   Feeling the rock beneath his feet,
And tracing through the cloud th' eternal Cause.

That is the heart for watchman true
Waiting to see what GOD will do,
As o'er the Church the gathering twilight falls :
   No more he strains his wistful eye,
   If chance the golden hours be nigh,
By youthful Hope seen beaming round her walls.

Forc'd from his shadowy paradise,
His thoughts to Heaven the steadier rise :
There seek his answer when the world reproves :
   Contented in his darkling round,
   If only he be faithful found,
When from the east th' eternal morning moves.

Note : The expression, "calm decay," is borrowed from a friend : by whose kind permission the following stanzas are here inserted.

TO THE RED-BREAST.

UNHEARD in summer's flaring ray,
   Pour forth thy notes, sweet singer,
Wooing the stillness of the autumn day:
   Bid it a moment linger,
     Nor fly
Too soon from winter's scowling eye.

The blackbird's song at even tide,
   And hers, who gay ascends,
Filling the heavens far and wide,
   Are sweet. But none so blends,
     As thine,
With calm decay, and peace divine.

LXXII.
TWENTY-SECOND SUNDAY AFTER TRINITY.

Lord, how oft shall my brother sin against me, and I forgive him? *St. Matthew* xviii. 21.

> W<small>HAT</small> liberty so glad and gay,
> As where the mountain boy,
> Reckless of regions far away,
> A prisoner lives in joy?
>
> The dreary sounds of crowded earth,
> The cries of camp or town,
> Never untun'd his lonely mirth,
> Nor drew his visions down.
>
> The snow-clad peaks of rosy light
> That meet his morning view,
> The thwarting cliffs that bound his sight,
> They bound his fancy too.

Twenty-second Sunday after Trinity.

Two ways alone his roving eye
    For aye may onward go,
Or in the azure deep on high,
    Or darksome mere below.

O blest restraint! more blessed range!
    Too soon the happy child
His nook of homely thought will change
    For life's seducing wild.

Too soon his alter'd day dreams shew
    This earth a boundless space,
With sun-bright pleasures to and fro
    Sporting in joyous race:

While of his narrowing heart each year,
    Heaven less and less will fill,
Less keenly, through his grosser ear,
    The tones of mercy thrill.

By our own niggard rule we try
    The hope to suppliants given;
We mete out love, as if our eye
    Saw to the end of heaven.

Twenty second Sunday after Trinity.

Yes, ransom'd sinner! wouldst thou know
 How often to forgive,
How dearly to embrace thy foe,
 Look where thou hop'st to live:

When thou hast told those isles of light,
 And fancied all beyond,
Whatever owns, in depth or height,
 Creation's wondrous bond;

Then in their solemn pageant learn
 Sweet mercy's praise to see:
Their Lord resign'd them all, to earn
 The bliss of pardoning thee.

LXXIII.
TWENTY-THIRD SUNDAY AFTER TRINITY.

Who shall change our vile body, that it may be fashioned like unto His glorious body, according to the working whereby He is able even to subdue all things unto Himself. Philippians iii. 21.

 RED o'er the forest glows the setting sun,
  The line of yellow light dies fast away
 That crown'd the eastern copse: and chill and dun
  Falls on the moor the brief November day.

 Now the tir'd hunter winds a parting note,
  And Echo bids good-night from every glade;
 Yet wait awhile, and see the calm leaves float
  Each to his rest beneath their parent shade.

 How like decaying life they seem to glide!
  And yet no second spring have they in store,
 But where they fall forgotten to abide,
  Is all their portion, and they ask no more.

Twenty-third Sunday after Trinity.

Soon o'er their heads blithe April airs shall sing,
   A thousand wild-flowers round them shall unfold,
The green buds glisten in the dews of Spring,
   And all be vernal rapture as of old.

Unconscious they in waste oblivion lie,
   In all the world of busy life around
No thought of them; in all the bounteous sky
   No drop, for them, of kindly influence found.

Man's portion is to die and rise again—
   Yet he complains, while these unmurmuring part
With their sweet lives, as pure from sin and stain,
   As his when Eden held his virgin heart.

And haply half unblam'd his murmuring voice
   Might sound in heaven, were all his second life
Only the first renew'd—the heathen's choice,
   A round of listless joy and weary strife.

For dreary were this earth, if earth were all,
   Though brighten'd oft by dear affection's kiss;—
Who for the spangles wears the funeral pall?
   But catch a gleam beyond it, and 'tis bliss.

Twenty-third Sunday after Trinity.

Heavy and dull this frame of limbs and heart,
    Whether slow creeping on cold earth, or borne
On lofty steed, or loftier prow, we dart
    O'er wave or field: yet breezes laugh to scorn

Our puny speed, and birds, and clouds in heaven,
    And fish, like living shafts that pierce the main,
And stars that shoot through freezing air at even —
    Who but would follow, might he break his chain?

And thou shalt break it soon; the groveling worm
    Shall find his wings, and soar as fast and free
As his transfigur'd Lord with lightning form
    And snowy vest—such grace He won for thee,

When from the grave He sprung at dawn of morn,
    And led through boundless air thy conquering road,
Leaving a glorious track, where saints new-born
    Might fearless follow to their blest abode.

But first, by many a stern and fiery blast
    The world's rude furnace must thy blood refine,
And many a gale of keenest woe be pass'd,
    Till every pulse beat true to airs divine,

Twenty third Sunday after Trinity

Till every limb obey the mounting soul,
  The mounting soul, the call by Jesus given.
He who the stormy heart can so control
  The laggard body soon will waft to heaven.

LXXIV.
TWENTY-FOURTH SUNDAY AFTER TRINITY.

The heart knoweth his own bitterness, and a stranger doth not intermeddle with his joy. *Proverbs* xiv. 10.

WHY should we faint and fear to live alone,
   Since all alone, so Heaven has will'd, we die [a],
Nor even the tenderest heart, and next our own,
   Knows half the reasons why we smile and sigh?

Each in his hidden sphere of joy or woe
   Our hermit spirits dwell, and range apart,
Our eyes see all around in gloom or glow—
   Hues of their own, fresh borrow'd from the heart.

And well it is for us our GOD should feel
   Alone our secret throbbings: so our prayer
May readier spring to Heaven, nor spend its zeal
   On cloud-born idols of this lower air.

       [a] Je mourrai seul. *Pascal.*

For if one heart in perfect sympathy
  Beat with another, answering love for love,
Weak mortals, all entranc'd, on earth would lie,
  Nor listen for those purer strains above.

Or what if Heaven for once its searching light
  Lent to some partial eye, disclosing all
The rude bad thoughts, that in our bosom's night
  Wander at large, nor heed Love's gentle thrall?

Who would not shun the dreary uncouth place?
  As if, fond leaning where her infant slept,
A mother's arm a serpent should embrace:
  So might we friendless live, and die unwept.

Then keep the softening veil in mercy drawn,
  Thou who canst love us, tho' Thou read us true;
As on the bosom of th' aerial lawn
  Melts in dim haze each coarse ungentle hue.

So too may soothing Hope thy leave enjoy
  Sweet visions of long sever'd hearts to frame:
Though absence may impair, or cares annoy,
  Some constant mind may draw us still the same.

Twenty fourth Sunday after Trinity.

We in dark dreams are tossing to and fro,
    Pine with regret, or sicken with despair,
The while she bathes us in her own chaste glow,
    And with our memory wings her own fond prayer.

O bliss of child-like innocence, and love
    Tried to old age! creative power to win,
And raise new worlds, where happy fancies rove,
    Forgetting quite this grosser world of sin.

Bright are their dreams, because their thoughts are clear,
    Their memory cheering: but th' earth-stained spright,
Whose wakeful musings are of guilt and fear,
    Must hover nearer earth, and less in light.

Farewell, for her, th' ideal scenes so fair—
    Yet not farewell her hope, since Thou hast deign'd,
Creator of all hearts! to own and share
    The woe of what Thou mad'st, and we have stain'd.

Thou know'st our bitterness—our joys are thine [b]—
    No stranger Thou to all our wanderings wild:

---

[b] Psalm xxxi. 8. Thou hast known my soul in adversities.

92 *Twenty-fourth Sunday after Trinity.*

Nor could we bear to think, how every line
  Of us, thy darken'd likeness and defil'd,

Stands in full sunshine of thy piercing eye,
  But that thou call'st us Brethren: sweet repose
Is in that word—the Lord who dwells on high
  Knows all, yet loves us better than He knows.

LXXV.
TWENTY-FIFTH SUNDAY AFTER TRINITY.

The hoary head is a crown of glory, if it be found in the way of righteousness. *Proverbs* xvi. 31.

THE bright hair'd morn is glowing
   O'er emerald meadows gay,
With many a clear gem strowing
   The early shepherd's way.
Ye gentle elves, by Fancy seen
   Stealing away with night
To slumber in your leafy screen,
   Tread more than airy light.

And see what joyous greeting
   The sun through heaven has shed,
Though fast yon shower be fleeting,
   His beams have faster sped.

For lo! above the western haze
   High towers the rainbow arch
In solid span of purest rays:
   How stately is its march!

Pride of the dewy morning!
   The swain's experienc'd eye
From thee takes timely warning,
   Nor trusts the gorgeous sky.
For well he knows, such dawnings gay
   Bring noons of storm and shower,
And travellers linger on the way
   Beside the sheltering bower.

Even so, in hope and trembling,
   Should watchful shepherd view
His little lambs assembling,
   With glance both kind and true;
'Tis not the eye of keenest blaze,
   Nor the quick-swelling breast,
That soonest thrills at touch of praise—
   These do not please him best.

But voices low and gentle,
   And timid glances shy,

That seem for aid parental
    To sue all wistfully,
Still pressing, longing to be right,
    Yet fearing to be wrong—
In these the Pastor dares delight,
    A lamb-like, Christ-like throng.

These in Life's distant even
    Shall shine serenely bright,
As in th' autumnal heaven
    Mild rainbow tints at night,
When the last shower is stealing down,
    And ere they sink to rest,
The sun-beams weave a parting crown
    For some sweet woodland nest.

The promise of the morrow
    Is glorious on that eve,
Dear as the holy sorrow
    When good men cease to live.
When brightening ere it die away
    Mounts up their altar-flame,
Still tending with intenser ray
    To Heaven whence first it came.

Say not it dies, that glory,
  'Tis caught unquench'd on high,
Those saintlike brows so hoary
  Shall wear it in the sky.
No smile is like the smile of death,
  When all good musings past
Rise wafted with the parting breath,
  The sweetest thought the last.

LXXVI.
LAST SUNDAY AFTER TRINITY.

Gather up the fragments that remain, that nothing be lost.
St. John vi. 12.

WILL God indeed with fragments bear,
Snatch'd late from the decaying year?
Or can the Saviour's blood endear
    The dregs of a polluted life?
When down th' o'erwhelming current tost,
Just ere he sink for ever lost,
The sailor's untried arms are cross'd
In agonizing prayer, will Ocean cease her strife?

Sighs that exhaust but not relieve,
Heart-rending sighs, O spare to heave
A bosom freshly taught to grieve
    For lavish'd hours and love mispent!

Last Sunday after Trinity

Now through her round of holy thought
The Church our annual steps has brought,
But we no holy fire have caught—
Back on the gaudy world our wilful eyes were bent.

Too soon th' ennobling carols, pour'd
To hymn the birth-night of the LORD,
Which duteous Memory should have stor'd
    For thankful echoing all the year—
Too soon those airs have pass'd away;
Nor long within the heart would stay
The silence of CHRIST's dying day,
Profan'd by worldly mirth, or scar'd by worldly fear.

Some strain of hope and victory
On Easter wings might lift us high;
A little while we sought the sky:
    And when the SPIRIT's beacon fires
On every hill began to blaze,
Lightening the world with glad amaze,
Who but must kindle while they gaze?
But faster than she soars, our earth-bound Fancy tires.

Nor yet for these, nor all the rites,
By which our Mother's voice invites

Last Sunday after Trinity.

Our GOD to bless our home delights,
    And sweeten every secret tear :—
The funeral dirge, the marriage vow,
The hallow'd font where parents bow,
And now elate and trembling now
To the Redeemer's feet their new-found treasures bear :—

Not for the Pastor's gracious arm
Stretch'd out to bless—a Christian charm
To dull the shafts of worldly harm :—
    Nor, sweetest, holiest, best of all,
For the dear feast of JESUS dying,
Upon that altar ever lying,
Where souls with sacred hunger sighing
Are call'd to sit and eat, while angels prostrate fall :—

No, not for each and all of these,
Have our frail spirits found their ease.
The gale that stirs th' autumnal trees
    Seems tun'd as truly to our hearts
As when, twelve weary months ago,
'Twas moaning bleak, so high and low,
You would have thought Remorse and Woe
Had taught the innocent air their sadly thrilling parts.

Is it, CHRIST'S light is too divine,
We dare not hope like Him to shine?
But see, around His dazzling shrine
    Earth's gems the fire of Heaven have caught;
Martyrs and saints—each glorious day
Dawning in order on our way—
Remind us, how our darksome clay
May keep th' ethereal warmth our new Creator brought.

These we have scorn'd, O false and frail!
And now once more th' appalling tale,
How love divine may woo and fail,
    Of our lost year in heaven is told—
What if as far our life were past,
Our weeks all number'd to the last,
With time and hope behind us cast,
And all our work to do with palsied hands and cold?

O watch and pray ere Advent dawn!
For thinner than the subtlest lawn
'Twixt thee and death the veil is drawn.
    But Love too late can never glow:

The scatter'd fragments Love can glean,
Refine the dregs, and yield us clean
To regions where one thought serene
Breathes sweeter than whole years of sacrifice below.

LXXVII.
ST. ANDREW'S DAY.

He first findeth his own brother Simon, and saith unto him, We have found the Messias; and he brought him unto Jesus. *St. John* i. 42.

WHEN brothers part for manhood's race,
   What gift may most endearing prove
To keep fond memory in her place,
   And certify a brother's love?

'Tis true, bright hours together told,
   And blissful dreams in secret shar'd,
Serene or solemn, gay or bold,
   Shall last in fancy unimpair'd.

Even round the death-bed of the good
   Such dear remembrances will hover,
And haunt us with no vexing mood
   When all the cares of earth are over.

St. Andrew's Day.

But yet our craving spirits feel,
   Fancy with all her dreams must die,
And seek a surer pledge—a seal
   Of love to last eternally.

Who art thou, that would'st grave thy name
   Thus deeply in a brother's heart?
Look on this saint, and learn to frame
   Thy love-charm with true Christian art.

First seek thy Saviour out, and dwell
   Beneath the shadow of his roof,
Till thou have scann'd his features well,
   And known Him for the Christ by proof;

Such proof as they are sure to find,
   Who spend with him their happy days,
Clean hands, and a self-ruling mind
   Ever in tune for love and praise.

Then, potent with the spell of heaven,
   Go, and thine erring brother gain,
Entice him home to be forgiven,
   Till he, too, see his Saviour plain.

Or, if before thee in the race,
　　Urge him with thine advancing tread
Till, like twin stars, with even pace
　　Each lucid course be duly sped.

No fading frail memorial give
　　To soothe his soul when thou art gone,
But wreaths of hope for aye to live,
　　And thoughts of good together done.

That so, before the judgment-seat,
　　Though chang'd and glorified each face,
Not unremember'd ye may meet
　　For endless ages to embrace.

LXXVIII.
ST. THOMAS' DAY.

Thomas, because thou hast seen me, thou hast believed: blessed are they that have not seen, and yet have believed. *St. John* xx. 29.

WE were not by when Jesus came [a],
    But round us, far and near,
We see his trophies, and his name
    In choral echoes hear.
In a fair ground our lot is cast,
As in the solemn week that past,
While some might doubt, but all ador'd [b],
Ere the whole widow'd Church had seen her risen Lord.

Slowly, as then, His bounteous hand
    The golden chain unwinds,

---

[a] St. John xx. 24. Thomas, one of the twelve, called Didymus, was not with them when Jesus came.

[b] St. Matt. xxviii. 17. When they saw him, they worshipped him: but some doubted.

St. Thomas' Day.

Drawing to Heaven with gentlest band
    Wise hearts and loving minds.
Love sought him first—at dawn of morn c
From her sad couch she sprang forlorn,
    She sought to weep with Thee alone,
And saw thine open grave, and knew that Thou wert gone.

Reason and Faith at once set out d
    To search the SAVIOUR's tomb;
Faith faster runs, but waits without,
    As fearing to presume
Till Reason enter in, and trace
Christ's relics round the holy place—
"Here lay His limbs, and here His sacred head,
"And who was by, to make his new-forsaken bed?"

Both wonder, one believes—but while
    They muse on all at home,
No thought can tender Love beguile
    From Jesus' grave to roam.

c St. Mary Magdalen's visit to the sepulchre.
d St. Peter and St. John.

Weeping she stays till He appear—
Her witness first the Church must hear—
All joy to souls that can rejoice
With her at earliest call of His dear gracious voice.

Joy too to those, who love to talk
  In secret how He died,
Though with seal'd eyes awhile they walk,
  Nor see Him at their side;
Most like the faithful pair are they,
Who once to Emmaus took their way,
Half darkling, till their Master shed
His glory on their souls, made known in breaking
  bread.

Thus, ever brighter and more bright,
  On those he came to save
The Lord of new-created light
  Dawn'd gradual from the grave:
Till pass'd th' enquiring daylight hour,
And with clos'd door in silent bower
The Church in anxious musing sate,
As one who for redemption still had long to wait.

Then, gliding through th' unopening door,
    Smooth without step or sound,
"Peace to your souls," He said—no more—
    They own him, kneeling round.
Eye, ear, and hand, and loving heart,
Body and soul in every part,
Successive made His witnesses that hour,
Cease not in all the world to shew his saving power.

Is there, on earth, a spirit frail,
    Who fears to take their word,
Scarce daring, through the twilight pale,
    To think he sees the Lord?
With eyes too tremblingly awake
To bear with dimness for His sake?
Read and confess the hand divine
That drew thy likeness here so true in every line.

For all thy rankling doubts so sore,
    Love thou thy Saviour still,
Him for thy Lord and God adore,
    And ever do His will.
Though vexing thoughts may seem to last,
Let not thy soul be quite o'ercast;—

Soon will He shew thee all His wounds, and say,
"Long have I known thy name ᵉ—know thou my
"face alway."

ᵉ In Exodus xxxiii. 17. God says to Moses, "I know thee by name;" meaning, "I bear especial favour towards thee." Thus our Saviour speaks to St. Thomas by name in the place here referred to.

LXXIX.
THE CONVERSION OF ST. PAUL.

And he fell to the earth, and heard a voice saying unto him, Saul, Saul, why persecutest thou me? And he said, Who art thou, Lord? And the Lord said, I am Jesus whom thou persecutest. Acts ix. 4, 5.

THE midday sun, with fiercest glare,
Broods o'er the hazy, twinkling air;
   Along the level sand
The palm-tree's shade unwavering lies,
Just as thy towers, Damascus, rise
   To greet yon wearied band.

The leader of that martial crew
Seems bent some mighty deed to do,
   So steadily he speeds,
With lips firm clos'd and fixed eye,
Like warrior when the fight is nigh,
   Nor talk nor landscape heeds.

The Conversion of St. Paul.

What sudden blaze is round him pour'd,
As though all heaven's refulgent hoard
    In one rich glory shone?
One moment—and to earth he falls:
What voice his inmost heart appals?—
    Voice heard by him alone.

For to the rest both words and form
Seem lost in lightning and in storm,
    While Saul, in wakeful trance,
Sees deep within that dazzling field
His persecuted Lord reveal'd
    With keen yet pitying glance:

And hears the meek upbraiding call
As gently on his spirit fall
    As if th' Almighty Son
Were prisoner yet in this dark earth,
Nor had proclaim'd his royal birth,
    Nor his great power begun.

" Ah wherefore persecut'st thou me?"
He heard and saw, and sought to free
    His strain'd eye from the sight:

But Heaven's high magic bound it there,
Still gazing, though untaught to bear
    Th' insufferable light.

" Who art thou, Lord?" he falters forth :—
So shall Sin ask of heaven and earth
    At the last awful day.
" When did we see thee suffering nigh [f],
" And pass'd thee with unheeding eye?
    " Great God of judgment, say!"

Ah! little dream our listless eyes
What glorious presence they despise,
    While, in our noon of life,
To power or fame we rudely press.—
Christ is at hand, to scorn or bless,
    Christ suffers in our strife.

And though heaven gate long since have clos'd,
And our dear Lord in bliss repos'd
    High above mortal ken,

---

[f] St. Matthew xxv. 44.

To every ear in every land
(Though meek ears only understand)
   He speaks as He did then.

" Ah wherefore persecute ye me ?
" 'Tis hard, ye so in love should be
   " With your own endless woe.
" Know, though at God's right hand I live,
" I feel each wound ye reckless give
   " To the least saint below.

" I in your care my brethren left,
" Not willing ye should be bereft
   " Of waiting on your Lord.
" The meanest offering ye can make—
" A drop of water—for love's sake ^g,
   " In Heaven, be sure, is stor'd."

O by those gentle tones and dear,
When Thou hast stay'd our wild career,
   Thou only hope of souls,

      ^g St. Matthew x. 41.

Ne'er let us cast one look behind,
But in the thought of Jesus find
    What every thought controuls.

As to thy last Apostle's heart
Thy lightning glance did then impart
    Zeal's never-dying fire,
So teach us on thy shrine to lay
Our hearts, and let them day by day
    Intenser blaze and higher.

And as each mild and winning note
(Like pulses that round harp-strings float,
    When the full strain is o'er)
Left lingering on his inward ear
Music, that taught, as death drew near,
    Love's lesson more and more:

So, as we walk our earthly round,
Still may the echo of that sound
    Be in our memory stor'd:
"Christians! behold your happy state:
"Christ is in these, who round you wait;
    "Make much of your dear Lord!"

LXXX.
THE PURIFICATION.

Blessed are the pure in heart; for they shall see God.
St. Matthew v. 3.

Bless'd are the pure in heart,
   For they shall see our God,
The secret of the Lord is theirs,
   Their soul is Christ's abode.

Might mortal thought presume
   To guess an angel's lay,
Such are the notes that echo through
   The courts of Heaven to-day.

Such the triumphal hymns
   On Sion's Prince that wait,
In high procession passing on
   Towards His temple-gate.

Give ear, ye kings—bow down,
　Ye rulers of the earth—
This, this is He; your Priest by grace,
　Your God and King by birth.

No pomp of earthly guards
　Attends with sword and spear,
And all-defying, dauntless look,
　Their monarch's way to clear:

Yet are there more with him
　Than all that are with you—
The armies of the highest Heaven,
　All righteous, good, and true.

Spotless their robes and pure,
　Dipp'd in the sea of light,
That hides the unapproached shrine
　From men's and angels' sight.

His throne, thy bosom blest,
　O Mother undefil'd—
That throne, if aught beneath the skies,
　Beseems the sinless child.

The Purification. 117

Lost in high thoughts, "whose son
"The wondrous Babe might prove,"
Her guileless husband walks beside,
Bearing the hallow'd dove;

Meet emblem of His vow,
Who, on this happy day,
His dove-like soul—best sacrifice—
Did on God's altar lay.

But who is he, by years
Bow'd, but erect in heart,
Whose prayers are struggling with his tears?
"Lord, let me now depart.

"Now hath thy servant seen
"Thy saving health, O Lord:
"'Tis time that I depart in peace,
"According to thy word."

Yet swells the pomp: one more
Comes forth to bless her God:
Full fourscore years, meek widow, she
Her heaven-ward way hath trod.

She who to earthly joys
So long had given farewell,
Now sees, unlook'd for, Heaven on earth,
Christ in His Israel.

Wide open from that hour
The temple-gates are set,
And still the saints rejoicing there
The holy Child have met.

Now count his train to-day,
And who may meet him, learn:
Him child-like sires, meek maidens find,
Where pride can nought discern.

Still to the lowly soul
He doth himself impart,
And for His cradle and His throne
Chooseth the pure in heart.

LXXXI.
ST. MATTHIAS' DAY.

Wherefore of these men, which have companied with us all the time that the Lord Jesus went in and out among us; beginning from the baptism of John, until that same day that he was taken up from us; must one be ordained to be a witness with us of his resurrection. *Acts* i. 21, 22.

WHO is God's chosen priest?
He, who on Christ stands waiting day and night,
Who trac'd His holy steps, nor ever ceas'd,
   From Jordan banks to Bethphage height:

Who hath learn'd lowliness
From his Lord's cradle, patience from His cross;
Whom poor men's eyes and hearts consent to bless;
   To whom, for Christ, the world is loss;

Who both in agony
Hath seen Him and in glory; and in both
Own'd Him divine, and yielded nothing loth,
   Body and soul, to live and die,

In witness of his Lord,
In humble following of his Saviour dear:
This is the man to wield th' unearthly sword,
    Warring unharm'd with sin and fear.

    But who can e'er suffice—
What mortal—for this more than angels' task,
Winning or losing souls, Thy life-blood's price?
    The gift were too divine to ask,

    But Thou hast made it sure
By Thy dear promise to Thy Church and Bride,
That Thou, on earth, would'st aye with her endure,
    Till earth to Heaven be purified.

    Thou art her only spouse,
Whose arm supports her, on whose faithful breast
Her persecuted head she meekly bows,
    Sure pledge of her eternal rest.

    Thou, her unerring guide,
Stayest her fainting steps along the wild;
Thy mark is on the bowers of lust and pride,
    That she may pass them undefil'd.

St. Matthias' Day.

  Who then, uncall'd by Thee,
Dare touch thy spouse, thy very self below?
Or who dare count him summon'd worthily,
  Except thine hand and seal he shew?

  Where can thy seal be found,
But on the chosen seed, from age to age
By thine anointed heralds duly crown'd,
  As kings and priests thy war to wage?

  Then fearless walk we forth,
Yet full of trembling, messengers of God;
Our warrant sure, but doubting of our worth,
  By our own shame alike and glory aw'd.

  Dread Searcher of the hearts,
Thou who didst seal by thy descending Dove
Thy servant's choice, O help us in our parts,
  Else helpless found, to learn and teach thy love.

LXXXII.
THE ANNUNCIATION OF THE BLESSED VIRGIN MARY.

And the Angel came in unto her, and said, Hail, thou that art highly favoured, the Lord is with thee, blessed art thou among women. St. Luke i. 28.

OH Thou who deign'st to sympathize
With all our frail and fleshly ties,
    Maker yet Brother dear,
Forgive the too presumptuous thought,
If, calming wayward grief, I sought
    To gaze on Thee too near.

Yet sure 'twas not presumption, Lord,
'Twas thine own comfortable word
    That made the lesson known:
Of all the dearest bonds we prove,
Thou countest sons' and mothers' love
    Most sacred, most thine own.

The Annunciation.

When wandering here a little span,
Thou took'st on Thee to rescue man,
    Thou hadst no earthly sire :
That wedded love we prize so dear,
As if our heaven and home were here,
    It lit in Thee no fire.

On no sweet sister's faithful breast
Wouldst thou thine aching forehead rest,
    On no kind brother lean :
But who, O perfect filial heart,
E'er did like Thee a true son's part,
    Endearing, firm, serene?

Thou wept'st, meek maiden, mother mild,
Thou wept'st upon thy sinless child,
    Thy very heart was riven :
And yet, what mourning matron here
Would deem thy sorrows bought too dear
    By all on this side Heaven?

A son that never did amiss,
That never sham'd his mother's kiss,
    Nor cross'd her fondest prayer :

Even from the tree he deign'd to bow
For her his agonized brow,
 Her, his sole earthly care.

Ave Maria! blessed Maid!
Lily of Eden's fragrant shade,
 Who can express the love
That nurtur'd thee so pure and sweet,
Making thy heart a shelter meet
 For Jesus' holy Dove?

Ave Maria! Mother blest,
To whom caressing and caress'd,
 Clings the Eternal Child;
Favour'd beyond Archangels' dream,
When first on thee with tenderest gleam
 Thy new-born Saviour smil'd:—

Ave Maria! Thou whose name
All but adoring love may claim,
 Yet may we reach thy shrine;
For He, thy Son and Saviour, vows
To crown all lowly lofty brows
 With love and joy like thine.

The Annunciation.

Bless'd is the womb that bare Him—bless'd ʰ
The bosom where his lips were press'd,
    But rather bless'd are they
Who hear his word and keep it well,
The living homes where Christ shall dwell,
    And never pass away.

ʰ St. Luke xi. 27, 28.

LXXXIII.
ST. MARK'S DAY.

And the contention was so sharp between them, that they departed asunder the one from the other. *Acts* xv. 39.

Compare 2 *Timothy* iv. 11. Take Mark, and bring him with thee, for he is profitable to me for the ministry.

OH! who shall dare in this frail scene
On holiest happiest thoughts to lean,
    On Friendship, Kindred, or on Love?
Since not Apostles' hands can clasp
Each other in so firm a grasp,
    But they shall change and variance prove.

Yet deem not, on such parting sad
Shall dawn no welcome dear and glad:
    Divided in their earthly race,
Together at the glorious goal,
Each leading many a rescu'd soul,
    The faithful champions shall embrace.

St. Mark's Day.

For even as those mysterious Four,
Who the bright whirling wheels upbore
    By Chebar in the fiery blast [1],
So, on their tasks of love and praise
The saints of God their several ways
    Right onward speed, yet join at last.

And sometimes even beneath the moon
The Saviour gives a gracious boon,
    When reconciled Christians meet,
And face to face, and heart to heart,
High thoughts of holy love impart
    In silence meek, or converse sweet.

Companion of the Saints! 'twas thine
To taste that drop of peace divine,
    When the great soldier of thy Lord
Call'd thee to take his last farewell,
Teaching the Church with joy to tell
    The story of your love restor'd.

---

[1] Ezekiel i. 9. They turned not when they went—they went every one straight forward.

O then the glory and the bliss,
When all that pain'd or seem'd amiss
    Shall melt with earth and sin away!
When saints beneath their Saviour's eye,
Fill'd with each other's company,
    Shall spend in love th' eternal day.

LXXXIV.
ST. PHILIP AND ST. JAMES.

Let the brother of low degree rejoice in that he is exalted: but the rich, in that he is made low. St. James i. 9, 10.

DEAR is the morning gale of spring,
    And dear th' autumnal eve;
But few delights can summer bring
    A Poet's crown to weave.

Her bowers are mute, her fountains dry,
    And ever Fancy's wing
Speeds from beneath her cloudless sky
    To autumn or to spring.

Sweet is the infant's waking smile,
    And sweet the old man's rest—
But middle age by no fond wile,
    No soothing calm is blest.

Still in the world's hot restless gleam
    She plies her weary task,
While vainly for some pleasant dream
    Her wandering glances ask.—

O shame upon thee, listless heart,
    So sad a sigh to heave,
As if thy SAVIOUR had no part
    In thoughts, that make thee grieve.

As if along His lonesome way
    He had not borne for thee
Sad languors through the summer day,
    Storms on the wintry sea.

Youth's lightning flash of joy secure
    Pass'd seldom o'er His spright,—
A well of serious thought and pure,
    Too deep for earthly light.

No spring was His—no fairy gleam—
    For He by trial knew
How cold and bare what mortals dream,
    To worlds where all is true.

St. Philip and St. James.

Then grudge not thou the anguish keen
    Which makes thee like thy LORD,
And learn to quit with eye serene
    Thy youth's ideal hoard.

Thy treasur'd hopes and raptures high—
    Unmurmuring let them go,
Nor grieve the bliss should quickly fly
    Which CHRIST disdain'd to know.

Thou shalt have joy in sadness soon;
    The pure, calm hope be thine,
Which brightens, like the eastern moon,
    As days wild lights decline.

Thus souls, by nature pitch'd too high,
    By sufferings plung'd too low,
Meet in the Church's middle sky,
    Half way 'twixt joy and woe,

To practise there the soothing lay
    That sorrow best relieves:
Thankful for all God takes away,
    Humbled by all He gives.

LXXXV.
ST. BARNABAS.

The Son of consolation, a Levite. *Acts* iv. 36.

THE world's a room of sickness, where each heart
   Knows its own anguish and unrest;
The truest wisdom there, and noblest art,
   Is his, who skills of comfort best;
Whom by the softest step and gentlest tone
     Enfeebled spirits own,
   And love to raise the languid eye,
When, like an angel's wing, they feel him fleeting by:—

Feel only—for in silence gently gliding
   Fain would he shun both ear and sight,
'Twixt Prayer and watchful Love his heart dividing,
   A nursing father day and night.

St. Barnabas.

Such were the tender arms, where cradled lay
    In her sweet natal day
  The Church of JESUS; such the love
He to his chosen taught for His dear widow'd Dove.

Warm'd underneath the Comforter's safe wing
    They spread th' endearing warmth around:
Mourners, speed here your broken hearts to bring,
    Here healing dews and balms abound:
Here are soft hands that cannot bless in vain,
    By trial taught your pain:
  Here loving hearts, that daily know
The heavenly consolations they on you bestow.

Sweet thoughts are theirs, that breathe serenest calms,
  Of holy offerings timely paid [a],
Of fire from Heaven to bless their votive alms
  And passions on GOD's altar laid.
The world to them is clos'd and now they shine
    With rays of love divine,

---

[a] Acts iv. 37. Having land, he sold it, and brought the money, and laid it at the Apostles' feet.

Through darkest nooks of this dull earth
Pouring, in showery times, their glow of "quiet
"mirth."

New hearts before their Saviour's feet to lay,
  This is their first their dearest joy:
Their next, from heart to heart to clear the way [a]
  For mutual love without alloy:
Never so blest, as when in JESUS' roll
    They write some hero-soul,
  More pleas'd upon his brightening road
To wait, than if their own with all his radiance glow'd.

O happy spirits, mark'd by God and man
  Their messages of love to bear,[b]
What though long since in Heaven your brows began
  The genial amarant wreath to wear,
And in th' eternal leisure of calm love
    Ye banquet there above,
  Yet in your sympathetic heart
We and our earthly griefs may ask and hope a part.

---

[a] Acts ix. 27. Barnabas took him, and brought him (Saul) to the Apostles.

[b] Acts xi. 22. xiii. 2.

Comfort's true sons! amid the thoughts of down
   That strew your pillow of repose,
Sure 'tis one joy to muse, how ye unknown
   By sweet remembrance soothe our woes,
And how the spark ye lit, of heavenly cheer,
     Lives in our embers here,
   Where'er the Cross is borne with smiles,
Or lighten'd secretly by Love's endearing wiles :

Where'er one Levite in the temple keeps
   The watch-fire of his midnight prayer,
Or issuing thence, the eyes of mourners steeps
   In heavenly balm, fresh gather'd there ;
Thus saints, that seem to die in earth's rude strife,
     Only win double life :
   They have but left our weary ways
To live in memory here, in heaven by love and praise.

LXXXVI.
ST. JOHN BAPTIST'S DAY.

Behold, I will send you Elijah the prophet before the great and terrible day of the Lord : and he shall turn the heart of the fathers unto the children, and the hearts of the children to the fathers. *Malachi* iv. 4, 5.

    TWICE in her season of decay
  The fallen Church hath felt Elijah's eye
    Dart from the wild its piercing ray :
Not keener burns, in the chill morning sky,
      The herald star,
      Whose torch afar
  Shadows and boding night-birds fly.

    Methinks we need him once again,
That favour'd seer—but where shall he be found ?
    By Cherith's side we seek in vain,
In vain on Carmel's green and lonely mound :
      Angels no more
      From Sinai soar,
  On his celestial errands bound.

St. John Baptist's Day.

But wafted to her glorious place
By harmless fire, among the ethereal thrones,
   His spirit with a dear embrace
Thee the lov'd harbinger of Jesus owns,
      Well-pleas'd to view
      Her likeness true,
And trace, in thine, her own deep tones.

Deathless himself, he joys with thee
To commune how a faithful martyr dies,
   And in the blest could envy be,
He would behold thy wounds with envious eyes
      Star of our morn,
      Who yet unborn [c]
Didst warn us where the Christ should rise.

Now resting from your jealous care
For sinners, such as Eden cannot know,
   Ye pour for us your mingled prayer,
No anxious fear to damp Affection's glow.
      Love draws a cloud
      From you to shroud
Rebellion's mystery here below.

---

[c] St. Luke i. 44. The Babe leaped in her womb for joy.

And since we see, and not afar,
The twilight of the great and dreadful day,
   Why linger, till Elijah's car
Stoop from the clouds? Why sleep ye? rise and pray,
      Ye heralds seal'd
      In camp or field
   Your Saviour's banner to display.

Where is the love the Baptist taught,
The soul unswerving and the fearless tongue?
   The much-enduring wisdom, sought
By lonely prayer the haunted rocks among?
      Who counts it gain [d]
      His light should wane,
   So the whole world to Jesus throng?

Thou Spirit who the Church didst lend
Her eagle wings, to shelter in the wild [e],
   We pray thee, ere the Judge descend,
With flames like these, all bright and undefil'd,
      Her watchfires light,
      To guide aright
   Our weary souls, by earth beguil'd.

---

[d] St. John iii. 30. He must increase, but I must decrease. Revelations xii. 14.

St. John Baptist's Day.

So glorious let thy Pastors shine,
That by their speaking lives the world may learn
    First filial duty, then divine ᶠ,
That sons to parents, all to Thee may turn;
        And ready prove
        In fires of love,
    At sight of Thee, for aye to burn.

ᶠ Malachi iv. 6. He shall turn the heart of the fathers to the children, and the heart of the children to their fathers.

St. Luke i. 17. To turn the hearts of the fathers to the children, and the disobedient to the wisdom of the just; to make ready a people prepared for the Lord.

LXXXVII.
ST. PETER'S DAY.

When Herod would have brought him out, the same night Peter was sleeping. *Acts* xii. 6.

THOU thrice denied, yet thrice belov'd [g],
    Watch by thine own forgiven friend;
In sharpest perils faithful prov'd,
    Let his soul love thee to the end.

The prayer is heard—else why so deep
    His slumber on the eve of death?
And wherefore smiles he in his sleep
    As one who drew celestial breath?

He loves and is belov'd again—
    Can his soul choose but be at rest?
Sorrow hath fled away, and Pain
    Dares not invade the guarded nest.

       [g] St. John xxi. 15, 16, 17.

St. Peter's Day.

He dearly loves, and not alone:
   For his wing'd thoughts are soaring high
Where never yet frail heart was known
   To breathe in vain affection's sigh.

He loves and weeps—but more than tears
   Have seal'd thy welcome and his love—
One look lives in him, and endears
   Crosses and wrongs where'er he rove:

That gracious chiding look [b], Thy call
   To win him to himself and Thee,
Sweetening the sorrow of his fall
   Which else were ru'd too bitterly.

Even through the veil of sleep it shines,
   The memory of that kindly glance;—
The Angel watching by divines
   And spares awhile his blissful trance.

Or haply to his native lake
   His vision wafts him back, to talk
With JESUS, ere his flight he take,
   As in that solemn evening walk,

[b] St. Luke xxii. 61.

When to the bosom of his friend,
    The Shepherd, He whose name is Good,
Did His dear lambs and sheep commend,
    Both bought and nourish'd with His blood:

Then laid on him th' inverted tree,
    Which firm embrac'd with heart and arm,
Might cast o'er hope and memory,
    O'er life and death, its awful charm.

With brightening heart he bears it on,
    His passport thro' th' eternal gates,
To his sweet home—so nearly won,
    He seems, as by the door he waits,

The unexpressive notes to hear
    Of angel song and angel motion,
Rising and falling on the ear
    Like waves in Joy's unbounded ocean.—

His dream is chang'd—the Tyrant's voice
    Calls to that last of glorious deeds—
But as he rises to rejoice,
    Not Herod but an Angel leads.

St Peter's Day.

He dreams he sees a lamp flash bright,
    Glancing around his prison room—
But 'tis a gleam of heavenly light
    That fills up all the ample gloom.

The flame, that in a few short years
    Deep through the chambers of the dead
Shall pierce, and dry the fount of tears,
    Is waving o'er his dungeon-bed.

Touch'd he upstarts—his chains unbind—
    Through darksome vault, up massy stair,
His dizzy, doubting footsteps wind
    To freedom and cool moonlight air.

Then all himself, all joy and calm,
    Though for a while his hand forego,
Just as it touch'd, the martyr's palm,
    He turns him to his task below;

The pastoral staff, the keys of heaven,
    To wield awhile in grey-hair'd might,
Then from his cross to spring forgiven,
    And follow JESUS out of sight.

LXXXVIII.
ST. JAMES'S DAY.

Ye shall indeed drink of my cup, and be baptized with the baptism that I am baptized with : but to sit on my right hand and on my left is not mine to give, but it shall be given to them for whom it is prepared of my Father. *St. Matthew* xx. 23.

SIT down and take thy fill of joy
   At God's right hand, a bidden guest,
Drink of the cup that cannot cloy,
   Eat of the bread that cannot waste.
O great Apostle! rightly now
   Thou readest all thy Saviour meant,
What time His grave yet gentle brow
   In sweet reproof on thee was bent.

"Seek ye to sit enthron'd by me?
   " Alas! ye know not what ye ask,
The first in shame and agony,
   " The lowest in the meanest task—

St. James's Day.

" This can ye be? and can ye drink
  " The cup that I in tears must steep,
" Nor from the whelming waters shrink
  " That o'er me roll so dark and deep?"

" We can—thine are we, dearest Lord,
  " In glory and in agony,
" To do and suffer all Thy word;
  " Only be Thou for ever nigh :"
" Then be it so—my cup receive,
  " And of my woes baptismal taste :
" But for the crown, that angels weave
  " For those next me in glory plac'd,

" I give it not by partial love ;
  " But in my Father's book are writ
" What names on earth shall lowliest prove
  " That they in Heaven may highest sit."
Take up the lesson, O my heart ;
  Thou Lord of meekness, write it there,
Thine own meek self to me impart,
  Thy lofty hope, thy lowly prayer :

If ever on the mount with Thee
  I seem to soar in vision bright,

With thoughts of coming agony [a]
  Stay Thou the too presumptuous flight :
Gently along the vale of tears
  Lead me from Tabor's sunbright steep,
Let me not grudge a few short years,
  With Thee tow'rd Heaven to walk and weep ;

Too happy, on my silent path,
  If now and then allow'd, with Thee
Watching some placid holy death,
  Thy secret work of love to see;
But oh most happy, should thy call,
  Thy welcome call, at last be given—
" Come where thou long hast stor'd thy all,
  " Come see thy place prepar'd in Heaven."

---

[a] St. Matthew xvii. 12. "Likewise shall also the Son of Man suffer of them." This was just after the transfiguration.

LXXXIX.
ST. BARTHOLOMEW.

Jesus answered and said unto him, Because I said unto thee, I saw thee under the fig-tree, believest thou? thou shalt see greater things than these. St. John i. 50.

HOLD up thy mirror to the sun,
   And thou shalt need an eagle's gaze,
So perfectly the polish'd stone
   Gives back the glory of his rays:

Turn it, and it shall paint as true
   The soft green of the vernal earth,
And each small flower of bashful hue,
   That closest hides its lowly birth.

Our mirror is a blessed book,
   Where out from each illumin'd page
We see one glorious Image look
   All eyes to dazzle and engage,

The Son of God: and that indeed
　We see Him, as He is, we know,
Since in the same bright glass we read
　The very life of things below.

Eye of God's word [b]! where'er we turn
　Ever upon us! thy keen gaze
Can all the depths of sin discern,
　Unravel every bosom's maze:

Who that has felt thy glance of dread
　Thrill through his heart's remotest cells,
About his path, about his bed,
　Can doubt what spirit in thee dwells?

[b] "The position before us is, that we ourselves, and such as we, are the very persons whom Scripture speaks of: and to whom, as men, in every variety of persuasive form, it makes its condescending though celestial appeal. The point worthy of observation is, to note how a book of the description and the compass which we have represented Scripture to be, possesses this versatility of power; *this eye, like that of a portrait, uniformly fixed upon us, turn where we will.*" Miller's Bampton Lectures, p. 128.

St. Bartholomew. 149

" What word is this? Whence know'st thou me?"
   All wondering cries the humbled heart,
To hear thee that deep mystery,
   The knowledge of itself, impart.

The veil is rais'd; who runs may read,
   By its own light the truth is seen,
And soon the Israelite indeed
   Bows down t' adore the Nazarene.

So did Nathanael, guileless man,
   At once, not shame-fac'd or afraid,
Owning Him God, who so could scan
   His musings in the lonely shade;

In his own pleasant fig-tree's shade,
   Which by his household fountain grew,
Where at noon-day his prayer he made,
   To know God better than he knew.

Oh! happy hours of heaven-ward thought!
   How richly crown'd! how well improv'd
In musing o'er the Law he taught,
   In waiting for the Lord he lov'd.

We must not mar with earthly praise
    What God's approving word hath seal'd;
Enough, if right our feeble lays
    Take up the promise He reveal'd;

"The child-like faith, that asks not sight,
    " Waits not for wonder or for sign,
" Believes, because it loves, aright—
    " Shall see things greater, things divine.

" Heaven to that gaze shall open wide,
    " And brightest angels to and fro
" On messages of love shall glide
    " 'Twixt God above, and Christ below."

So still the guileless man is blest,
    To him all crooked paths are straight,
Him on his way to endless rest
    Fresh, ever-growing strengths await [c].

God's witnesses, a glorious host,
    Compass him daily like a cloud;

---

[c] Psalm lxxxiv. 7. They shall go from strength to strength.

St. Bartholomew.

Martyrs and seers, the sav'd and lost,
Mercies and judgments cry aloud.

Yet shall to him the still small voice,
That first into his bosom found
A way, and fix'd his wavering choice,
Nearest and dearest ever sound.

XC.
ST. MATTHEW.

And after these things, He went forth and saw a publican named Levi, sitting at the receipt of custom, and He said unto him, Follow me : and he left all, rose up, and followed Him. *St. Luke* v. 27, 28.

Y E hermits blest, ye holy maids,
   The nearest heaven on earth,
Who talk with God in shadowy glades,
   Free from rude care and mirth ;
To whom some viewless teacher brings
   The secret lore of rural things,
The moral of each fleeting cloud and gale,
The whispers from above, that haunt the twilight vale :

Say, when in pity ye have gaz'd
   On the wreath'd smoke afar,
That o'er some town, like mist uprais'd,
   Hung hiding sun and star,

Then as ye turn'd your weary eye
To the green earth and open sky,
Were ye not fain to doubt how Faith could dwell
Amid that dreary glare, in this world's citadel?

But Love's a flower that will not die
   For lack of leafy screen,
And Christian Hope can cheer the eye
   That ne'er saw vernal green;
Then be ye sure that Love can bless
Even in this crowded loneliness,
Where ever-moving myriads seem to say,
Go—thou art nought to us, nor we to thee—away!

There are in this loud stunning tide
   Of human care and crime,
With whom the melodies abide
   Of th' everlasting chime;
Who carry music in their heart
Through dusky lane and wrangling mart,
Plying their daily task with busier feet,
Because their secret souls a holy strain repeat.

How sweet to them, in such brief rest
   As thronging cares afford,

In thought to wander, fancy-blest,
  To where their gracious Lord,
In vain, to win proud Pharisees,
  Spake, and was heard by fell disease ᵈ—
But not in vain, beside yon breezy lake,
Bade the meek Publican his gainful seat forsake:

At once he rose, and left his gold;
  His treasure and his heart
Transferr'd, where he shall safe behold
  Earth and her idols part;
While he beside his endless store
Shall sit, and floods unceasing pour
Of Christ's true riches o'er all time and space,
First angel of his Church, first steward of his Grace:

Nor can ye not delight to think ᵉ
  Where He vouchsaf'd to eat,
How the Most Holy did not shrink
  From touch of sinner's meat;
What worldly hearts and hearts impure
Went with him through the rich man's door,

ᵈ It seems from St. Matthew ix. 8, 9, that the calling of Levi took place immediately after the healing of the paralytic in the presence of the Pharisees.

ᵉ St. Matth. ix. 10.

That we might learn of Him lost souls to love,
And view his least and worst with hope to meet above.

These gracious lines shed Gospel light
   On Mammon's gloomiest cells,
As on some city's cheerless night
   The tide of sun-rise swells,
Till tower, and dome, and bridge-way proud
Are mantled with a golden cloud,
And to wise hearts this certain hope is given;
" No mist that man may raise, shall hide the eye of
" Heaven."

And oh! if even on Babel shine
   Such gleams of Paradise,
Should not their peace be peace divine,
   Who day by day arise
To look on clearer Heavens, and scan
The work of God untouch'd by man?
Shame on us, who about us Babel bear,
And live in Paradise, as if God was not there!

XCI.

ST. MICHAEL AND ALL ANGELS.

Are they not all ministering spirits, sent forth to minister for them who shall be heirs of salvation? Heb. i. 14.

Y E stars that round the Sun of righteousness
    In glorious order roll,
With harps for ever strung, ready to bless
    God for each rescu'd soul,
Ye eagle spirits, that build in light divine,
    Oh think of us to-day,
Faint warblers of this earth, that would combine
Our trembling notes with your accepted lay.

Your amaranth wreaths were earn'd; and homeward all,
    Flush'd with victorious might,

St Michael and all Angels. 157

Ye might have sped to keep high festival,
    And revel in the light;
But meeting us, weak worldlings, on our way,
    Tired ere the fight begun,
Ye turn'd to help us in th' unequal fray,
Remembering whose we were, how dearly won.

Remembering Bethlehem, and that glorious night
    When ye, who used to soar
Diverse along all space in fiery flight,
    Came thronging to adore
Your God new-born, and made a sinner's child;
    As if the stars should leave
Their stations in the far etherial wild,
And round the sun a radiant circle weave.

Nor less your lay of triumph greeted fair
    Our Champion and your King,
In that first strife, whence Satan in despair
    Sunk down on scathed wing:
Alone He fasted, and alone He fought;
    But when his toils were o'er,
Ye to the sacred Hermit duteous brought
Banquet and hymn, your Eden's festal store:

Ye too, when lowest in th' abyss of woe
      He plung'd to save his sheep,
Were leaning from your golden thrones to know
      The secrets of that deep:
But clouds were on his sorrow: one alone
      His agonizing call
Summon'd from Heaven, to still that bitterest groan,
And comfort Him, the Comforter of all.

Oh! highest favour'd of all Spirits create,
      (If right of thee we deem)
How didst thou glide on brightening wing elate
      To meet th' unclouded beam
Of Jesus from the couch of darkness rising!
      How swell'd thine anthem's sound,
With fear and mightier joy weak hearts surprising,
"Your God is risen, and may not here be found."

Pass a few days, and this dull darkling globe
      Must yield him from her sight;—
Brighter and brighter streams his glory-robe,
      And He is lost in light.
Then, when through yonder everlasting arch,
      Ye in innumerous choir

St. Michael and all Angels. 159

Pour'd, heralding Messiah's conquering march,
Linger'd around his skirts two forms of fire:

With us they staid, high warning to impart;
 " The Christ shall come again
" Even as He goes; with the same human heart,
 " With the same godlike train."—
Oh! jealous God! how could a sinner dare
 Think on that dreadful day,
But that with all thy wounds Thou wilt be there,
And all our angel friends to bring Thee on thy way?

Since to thy little ones is given such grace,
 That they who nearest stand
Alway to God in Heaven, and see His face,
 Go forth at his command,
To wait around our path in weal or woe,
 As erst upon our King,
Set thy baptismal seal upon our brow,
And waft us heaven-ward with enfolding wing:

Grant, Lord, that when around th' expiring world
 Our Seraph guardians wait,
While on her death-bed, ere to ruin hurl'd,
 She owns thee, all too late,

They to their charge may turn, and thankful see
    Thy mark upon us still;
Then all together rise, and reign with Thee,
And all their holy joy o'er contrite hearts fulfil!

XCII.
ST. LUKE.

Luke, the beloved physician, and Demas, greet you. *Colossians* iv. 14.

Demas hath forsaken me, having loved this present world. Only Luke is with me. 2 *Tim.* iv. 10, 11.

   T WO clouds before the summer gale
      In equal race fleet o'er the sky:
   Two flowers, when wintry blasts assail,
      Together pine, together die.

   But two capricious human hearts —
      No sage's rod may track their ways,
   No eye pursue their lawless starts
      Along their wild self-chosen maze.

   He only, by whose sovereign hand
      Even sinners for the evil day [a]
   Were made — who rules the world he plann'd,
      Turning our worst his own good way;

[a] Proverbs xvi. 4. The Lord hath made all things for himself, yea, even the wicked for the day of evil.

He only can the cause reveal,
    Why, at the same fond bosom fed,
Taught in the self-same lap to kneel
    Till the same prayer were duly said,

Brothers in blood and nurture too,
    Aliens in heart so oft should prove;
One lose, the other keep, Heaven's clue;
    One dwell in wrath, and one in love.

He only knows, — for He can read
    The mystery of the wicked heart,—
Why vainly oft our arrows speed
    When aim'd with most unerring art;

While from some rude and powerless arm
    A random shaft in season sent
Shall light upon some lurking harm,
    And work some wonder little meant.

Doubt we, how souls so wanton change,
    Leaving their own experienc'd rest?
Needs not around the world to range;
    One narrow cell may teach us best.

St. Luke.

Look in, and see Christ's chosen saint
    In triumph wear his Christ-like chain ;
No fear lest he should swerve or faint ;
    "His life is Christ, his death is gain [b]."

Two converts, watching by his side,
    Alike his love and greetings share ;
Luke the belov'd, the sick soul's guide,
    And Demas, nam'd in faltering prayer.

Pass a few years—look in once more—
    The saint is in his bonds again ;
Save that his hopes more boldly soar [c],
    He and his lot unchang'd remain.

But only Luke is with him now :—
    Alas! that even the martyr's cell,
Heaven's very gate, should scope allow
    For the false world's seducing spell.

[b] Philip. i. 21.

[c] In the Epistle to the Philippians, "I know that I shall continue with you all : I count not myself to have apprehended." i. 2; iii. 13.

In 2 Tim. "I have finished my course," etc. iv. 7, 8.

St. Luke.

'Tis sad—but yet 'tis well, be sure,
    We on the sight should muse awhile,
Nor deem our shelter all secure
    Even in the Church's holiest aisle.

Vainly before the shrine he bends,
    Who knows not the true pilgrim's part:
The martyr's cell no safety lends
    To him, who wants the martyr's heart.

But if there be, who follows Paul
    As Paul his Lord, in life and death,
Where'er an aching heart may call,
    Ready to speed and take no breath;

Whose joy is, to the wandering sheep
    To tell of the great Shepherd's love [d];
To learn of mourners while they weep
    The music that makes mirth above;

Who makes the Saviour all his theme.
    The Gospel all his pride and praise—

---

[d] The Gospel of St. Luke abounds most in such passages as the parable of the lost sheep, which display God's mercy to penitent sinners.

St. Luke.

   Approach : for thou canst feel the gleam
      That round the martyr's death-bed plays :

   Thou hast an ear for angels' songs,
      A breath the Gospel trump to fill,
   And taught by thee the Church prolongs
      Her hymns of high thanksgiving still [e].

   Ah! dearest mother, since too oft
      The world yet wins some Demas frail
   Even from thine arms, so kind and soft,
      May thy tried comforts never fail?

   When faithless ones forsake thy wing,
      Be it vouchsaf'd thee still to see
   Thy true, fond nurslings closer cling,
      Cling closer to their Lord and thee.

[e] The Christian hymns are all in St. Luke : the Magnificat, Benedictus, and Nunc Dimittis.

XCIII.
ST. SIMON AND ST. JUDE.

That ye should earnestly contend for the faith which was once delivered unto the saints. *St. Jude* 3.

SEEST thou, how tearful and alone,
   And drooping like a wounded dove,
The cross in sight, but Jesus gone,
   The widow'd Church is fain to rove?

Who is at hand that loves the Lord?
   Make haste and take her home, and bring
Thine household choir, in true accord
   Their soothing hymns for her to sing.

Soft on her fluttering heart shall breathe
   The fragrance of that genial isle,
There she may weave her funeral wreath,
   And to her own sad music smile.

[r] St. John xix. 26. Then saith He to the disciple, Behold thy mother : and from that hour that disciple took her to his own home.

St. Simon and St Jude.

The Spirit of the dying Son
   Is there, and fills the holy place
With records sweet of duties done,
   Of pardon'd foes, and cherish'd grace.

And as of old by two and two ^g
   His herald saints the Saviour sent
To soften hearts like morning dew,
   Where He to shine in mercy meant ;

So evermore He deems his name
   Best honour'd and His way prepar'd,
When watching by his altar-flame
   He sees his servants duly pair'd.

He loves when age and youth are met,
   Fervent old age and youth serene,
Their high and low in concord set
   For sacred song, Joy's golden mean.

He loves when some clear soaring mind
   Is drawn by mutual piety
To simple souls and unrefin'd,
   Who in life's shadiest covert lie.

        ^g St. Mark vi. 7.   St Luke x. 1.

Or if perchance a sadden'd heart
  That once was gay and felt the spring,
Cons slowly o'er its alter'd part,
  In sorrow and remorse to sing,

Thy gracious care will send that way
  Some spirit full of glee, yet taught
To bear the sight of dull decay,
  And nurse it with all pitying thought;

Cheerful as soaring lark, and mild
  As evening blackbird's full-ton'd lay,
When the relenting sun has smil'd
  Bright through a whole December day.

These are the tones to brace and cheer
  The lonely watcher of the fold,
When nights are dark, and foemen near,
  When visions fade and hearts grow cold.

How timely then a comrade's song
  Comes floating on the mountain air,
And bids thee yet be bold and strong—
  Fancy may die, but Faith is there.

XCIV.
ALL SAINTS' DAY.

Hurt not the earth, neither the sea, nor the trees, till we have sealed the servants of our God in their foreheads. *Revelations* vii. 3.

WHY blow'st thou not, thou wintry wind,
   Now every leaf is brown and sere,
And idly droops, to thee resign'd,
   The fading chaplet of the year?
Yet wears the pure aerial sky
Her summer veil, half drawn on high,
Of silvery haze, and dark and still
The shadows sleep on every slanting hill.

How quiet shews the woodland scene!
   Each flower and tree, its duty done,
Reposing in decay serene,
   Like weary men when age is won,

Such calm old age as conscience pure
And self-commanding hearts ensure,
Waiting their summons to the sky,
Content to live, but not afraid to die.

Sure if our eyes were purg'd to trace
 God's unseen armies hovering round,
We should behold by angels' grace
 The four strong winds of Heaven fast bound,
Their downward sweep a moment staid
On ocean cove and forest glade,
Till the last flower of autumn shed
Her funeral odours on her dying bed.

So in thine awful armoury, Lord,
 The lightnings of the judgment day
Pause yet awhile, in mercy stor'd,
 Till willing hearts wear quite away
Their earthly stains ; and spotless shine
On every brow in light divine
The cross by angel hands impress'd,
The seal of glory won and pledge of promis'd rest.

Little they dream, those haughty souls
 Whom empires own with bended knee,

What lowly fate their own controuls,
   Together link'd by Heaven's decree ;—
As bloodhounds hush their baying wild
To wanton with some fearless child,
So Famine waits, and War with greedy eyes,
Till some repenting heart be ready for the skies.

Think ye the spires that glow so bright
   In front of yonder setting sun,
Stand by their own unshaken might?
   No—where th' upholding grace is won.
We dare not ask, nor Heaven would tell,
But sure from many a hidden dell,
From many a rural nook unthought of there,
Rises for that proud world the saints' prevailing prayer.

On, champions blest, in Jesus' name,
   Short be your strife, your triumph full,
Till every heart have caught your flame,
   And lighten'd of the world's misrule
Ye soar those elder saints to meet,
Gather'd long since at Jesus' feet,
No world of passions to destroy,
Your prayers and struggles o'er, your task all praise
   and joy.

XCV.

HOLY COMMUNION.

O GOD of Mercy, God of Might,
How should pale sinners bear the sight,
If, as Thy power is surely here,
Thine open glory should appear?

For now thy people are allow'd
To scale the mount and pierce the cloud,
And Faith may feed her eager view
With wonders Sinai never knew.

Fresh from th' atoning sacrifice
The world's Creator bleeding lies,
That man, his foe, by whom He bled,
May take him for his daily bread.

Holy Communion. 173

O agony of wavering thought
When sinners first so near are brought!
" It is my Maker—dare I stay ?
" My Saviour—dare I turn away ?"

Thus while the storm is high within
'Twixt love of Christ and fear of sin,
Who can express the soothing charm,
To feel thy kind upholding arm,

My mother Church ? and hear thee tell
Of a world lost, yet lov'd so well,
That He, by whom the angels live,
His only Son for her would give [h].

And doubt we yet ? thou call'st again :
A lower still, a sweeter strain ;
A voice from Mercy's inmost shrine,
The very breath of Love divine.

---

[h] "God so loved the world, that He gave His only-begotten
" Son." See the sentences in the Communion Service, after the
Confession.

Whispering it says to each apart,
"Come unto me, thou trembling heart [i];"
And we must hope, so sweet the tone,
The precious words are all our own.

Hear them, kind Saviour—hear thy spouse
Low at thy feet renew her vows;
Thine own dear promise she would plead
For us her true though fallen seed.

She pleads by all thy mercies, told
Thy chosen witnesses of old,
Love's heralds sent to man forgiven,
One from the cross, and one from heaven [k].

This, of true Penitents the chief,
To the lost spirit brings relief,
Lifting on high th' adored name :—
"Sinners to save, Christ Jesus came [l]."

[i] Come unto me, all ye that travail, and are heavy laden, and I will refresh you.

[k] St. Paul and St. John.

[l] This is a faithful saying and worthy of all men to be received, That Christ Jesus came into the world to save sinners.

Holy Communion. 175

That, dearest of thy bosom friends,
Into the wavering heart descends:—
" What? down again? yet cheerful rise [m],
" Thine Intercessor never dies."

The eye of Faith, that waxes bright
Each moment by thine altar's light,
Sees them e'en now: they still abide
In mystery kneeling at our side;

And with them every spirit blest,
From realms of triumph or of rest,
From Him who saw creation's morn,
Of all thine angels eldest born,

To the poor babe, who died to-day,
Take part in our thanksgiving lay,
Watching the tearful joy and calm,
While sinners taste thine heavenly balm.

Sweet awful hour! the only sound
One gentle footstep gliding round,

[m] If any man sin, we have an Advocate with the Father, Jesus Christ the righteous.

Offering by turns on Jesus' part
The cross to every hand and heart.

Refresh us, Lord, to hold it fast;
Then when thy veil is drawn at last,
Let us depart where shadows cease,
With words of blessing and of peace.

XCVI.
HOLY BAPTISM.

Where is it, mothers learn their love?—
In every Church a fountain springs
O'er which th' eternal Dove
Hovers on softest wings.

What sparkles in that lucid flood
Is water, by gross mortals ey'd:
But seen by Faith, 'tis blood
Out of a dear friend's side.

A few calm words of faith and prayer,
A few bright drops of holy dew,
Shall work a wonder there
Earth's charmers never knew.

Holy Baptism.

O happy arms, where cradled lies,
   And ready for the Lord's embrace,
     That precious sacrifice,
       The darling of his grace!

Blest eyes, that see the smiling gleam
   Upon the slumbering features glow,
     When the life-giving stream
       Touches the tender brow!

Or when the holy cross is sign'd,
   And the young soldier duly sworn
     With true and fearless mind
       To serve the Virgin-born.

But happiest ye, who seal'd and blest
   Back to your arms your treasure take,
     With Jesus' mark impress'd
       To nurse for Jesus' sake:

To whom—as if in hallow'd air
   Ye knelt before some awful shrine—
     His innocent gestures wear
       A meaning half divine:

Holy Baptism.

By whom Love's daily touch is seen
  In strengthening form and freshening hue,
    In the fix'd brow serene,
      The deep yet eager view.—

Who taught thy pure and even breath
  To come and go with such sweet grace?
    Whence thy reposing Faith,
      Though in our frail embrace?

O tender gem, and full of Heaven!
  Not in the twilight stars on high,
    Not in moist flowers at even
      See we our God so nigh.

Sweet one, make haste and know Him too,
  Thine own adopting Father love,
    That like thine earliest dew
      Thy dying sweets may prove.

XCVII.
CATECHISM.

OH say not, dream not, heavenly notes
    To childish ears are vain,
That the young mind at random floats,
    And cannot reach the strain.

Dim or unheard, the words may fall,
    And yet the heaven-taught mind
May learn the sacred air, and all
    The harmony unwind.

Was not our Lord a little child,
    Taught by degrees to pray,
By father dear and mother mild
    Instructed day by day?

Catechism. 181

And lov'd He not of Heaven to talk
    With children in His sight,
To meet them in His daily walk,
    And to His arms invite?

What though around His throne of fire
    The everlasting chant
Be wafted from the seraph choir
    In glory jubilant?

Yet stoops He, ever pleas'd to mark
    Our rude essays of love,
Faint as the pipe of wakening lark,
    Heard by some twilight grove:

Yet is He near us, to survey
    These bright and order'd files,
Like spring-flowers in their best array,
    All silence and all smiles,

Save that each little voice in turn
    Some glorious truth proclaims,
What sages would have died to learn,
    Now taught by cottage dames.

And if some tones be false or low,
    What are all prayers beneath
But cries of babes, that cannot know
    Half the deep thought they breathe?

In His own words we Christ adore,
    But angels, as we speak,
Higher above our meaning soar
    Than we o'er children weak:

And yet His words mean more than they,
    And yet He owns their praise:
Why should we think, He turns away
    From infants' simple lays?

XCVIII.

CONFIRMATION.

THE shadow of th' Almighty's cloud
   Calm on the tents of Israel lay,
While drooping paus'd twelve banners proud,
   Till He arise and lead the way.

Then to the desert breeze unroll'd
   Cheerly the waving pennons fly,
Lion or eagle—each bright fold
   A lodestar to a warrior's eye.

So should thy champions, ere the strife,
   By holy hands o'er-shadow'd kneel,
So, fearless for their charmed life,
   Bear, to the end, thy Spirit's seal.

Steady and pure as stars that beam
  In middle heaven, all mist above,
Seen deepest in the frozen stream :—
  Such is their high courageous love.

And soft as pure, and warm as bright,
  They brood upon life's peaceful hour,
As if the Dove that guides their flight
  Shook from her plumes a downy shower.

Spirit of might and sweetness too!
  Now leading on the wars of God,
Now to green isles of shade and dew
  Turning the waste thy people trod;

Draw, Holy Ghost, thy seven-fold veil
  Between us and the fires of youth;
Breathe, Holy Ghost, thy freshening gale,
  Our fever'd brow in age to soothe.

And oft as sin and sorrow tire,
  The hallow'd hour do Thou renew,
When beckon'd up the awful choir
  By pastoral hands, toward Thee we drew;

Confirmation.

When trembling at the sacred rail
   We hid our eyes and held our breath,
Felt thee how strong, our hearts how frail,
   And long'd to own thee to the death.

For ever on our souls be trac'd
   That blessing dear, that dove-like hand,
A sheltering rock in Memory's waste,
   O'er-shadowing all the weary land.

XCIX.
MATRIMONY.

There is an awe in mortals' joy,
    A deep mysterious fear
Half of the heart will still employ,
    As if we drew too near
To Eden's portal, and those fires
That bicker round in wavy spires,
Forbidding, to our frail desires,
    What cost us once so dear.

We cower before th' heart-searching eye
    In rapture as in pain;
Even wedded Love, till Thou be nigh,
    Dares not believe her gain:
Then in the air she fearless springs,
The breath of Heaven beneath her wings,
And leaves her woodnotes wild, and sings
    A tun'd and measur'd strain.

Matrimony.

Ill fare the lay, though soft as dew
    And free as air it fall,
That, with thine altar full in view,
    Thy votaries would enthrall
To a foul dream, of heathen night,
Lifting her torch in Love's despite
And scaring, with base wildfire light,
    The sacred nuptial hall.

Far other strains, far other fires,
    Our marriage offering grace;
Welcome, all chaste and kind desires,
    With even matron pace
Approaching down the hallow'd aisle!
Where should ye seek Love's perfect smile,
But where your prayers were learn'd erewhile,
    In her own native place?

Where, but on His benignest brow,
    Who waits to bless you here?
Living, He own'd no nuptial vow,
    No bower to Fancy dear:
Love's very self—for Him no need
To nurse, on earth, the heavenly seed:

Yet comfort in His eye we read
    For bridal joy and fear.

'Tis He who clasps the marriage band,
    And fits the spousal ring,
Then leaves ye kneeling, hand in hand,
    Out of His stores to bring
His Father's dearest blessing, shed
Of old on Isaac's nuptial bed,
Now on the board before ye spread
    Of our all-bounteous King.

All blessings of the breast and womb,
    Of heaven and earth beneath,
Of converse high, and sacred home,
    Are yours, in life and death.
Only kneel on, nor turn away
From the pure shrine, where Christ to-day
Will store each flower, ye duteous lay,
    For an eternal wreath.

C.

VISITATION AND COMMUNION OF THE SICK.

O YOUTH and Joy, your airy tread
Too lightly springs by Sorrow's bed,
Your keen eye glances are too bright,
Too restless for a sick man's sight.
Farewell: for one short life we part:
I rather woo the soothing art,
Which only souls in sufferings tried
Bear to their suffering brethren's side.

Where may we learn that gentle spell?
Mother of Martyrs, thou canst tell!
Thou, who didst watch thy dying Spouse
With pierced hands and bleeding brows,
Whose tears from age to age are shed
O'er sainted sons untimely dead.
If e'er we charm a soul in pain,
Thine is the key-note of our strain.

Visitation and Communion of the Sick.

How sweet with thee to lift the latch
Where Faith has kept her midnight watch
Smiling on woe: with thee to kneel,
Where fix'd, as if one prayer could heal,
She listens, till her pale eye glow
With joy, wild health can never know,
And each calm feature, ere we read
Speaks, silently, thy glorious Creed.

Such have I seen: and while they pour'd
Their hearts in every contrite word,
How have I rather long'd to kneel
And ask of them sweet pardon's seal!
How blest the heavenly music brought
By thee to aid my faltering thought!
Peace ere we kneel, and when we cease
To pray, the farewell word is, "Peace."

I came again: the place was bright
"With something of celestial light"—
A simple altar by the bed
For high Communion meetly spread,
Chalice, and plate, and snowy vest.—
We ate and drank: then, calmly blest,

All mourners, one with dying breath,
We sate and talk'd of Jesus' death.

Once more I came : the silent room
Was veil'd in sadly-soothing gloom,
And ready for her last abode
The pale form like a lily shew'd,
By virgin fingers duly spread,
And priz'd for love of summer fled.
The light from those soft-smiling eyes
Had fleeted to its parent skies.

O soothe us, haunt us, night and day,
Ye gentle Spirits far away,
With whom we shar'd the cup of grace,
Then parted ; ye to Christ's embrace,
We to the lonesome world again,
Yet mindful of th' unearthly strain
Practis'd with you at Eden's door,
To be sung on, where angels soar,
With blended voices evermore.

CI.
BURIAL OF THE DEAD.

And when the Lord saw her, He had compassion on her, and said unto her, Weep not. And He came and touched the bier (and they that bare him stood still) and said, Young man, I say unto thee, Arise. *St. Luke* vii. 14, 15.

WHO says, the wan autumnal sun
    Beams with too faint a smile
To light up nature's face again,
And, though the year be on the wane,
    With thoughts of spring the heart beguile?

Waft him, thou soft September breeze,
    And gently lay him down
Within some circling woodland wall,
Where bright leaves, reddening ere they fall,
    Wave gaily o'er the waters brown.

And let some graceful arch be there
    With wreathed mullions proud,

Burial of the Dead.

With burnish'd ivy for its screen,
And moss, that glows as fresh and green
   As though beneath an April cloud.—

Who says the widow's heart must break,
   The childless mother sink?—
A kinder truer voice I hear,
Which even beside that mournful bier
   Whence parents' eyes would hopeless shrink,

Bids weep no more—O heart bereft,
   How strange, to thee, that sound!
A widow o'er her only son,
Feeling more bitterly alone
   The friends that press officious round.

Yet is the voice of comfort heard,
   For Christ hath touch'd the bier—
The bearers wait with wondering eye,
The swelling bosom dares not sigh,
   But all is still, 'twixt hope and fear.

Even such an awful soothing calm
   We sometimes see alight

On Christian mourners while they wait,
In silence, by some church-yard gate,
  Their summons to the holy rite.

And such the tones of love, which break
  The stillness of that hour,
Quelling th' embitter'd spirit's strife—
"The Resurrection and the Life
  "Am I: believe, and die no more."—

Unchang'd that voice—and though not yet
  The dead sit up and speak,
Answering its call; we gladlier rest
Our darlings on earth's quiet breast,
  And our hearts feel they must not break.

Far better they should sleep awhile
  Within the church's shade,
Nor wake, until new heaven, new earth,
Meet for their new immortal birth
  For their abiding place be made,

Then wander back to life, and lean
  On our frail love once more.

Burial of the Dead.

'Tis sweet, as year by year we lose
Friends out of sight, in faith to muse
  How grows in Paradise our store.

Then pass, ye mourners, cheerly on,
    Through prayer unto the tomb,
Still, as ye watch life's falling leaf,
Gathering from every loss and grief
  Hope of new spring and endless home.

Then cheerly to your work again
    With hearts new-brac'd and set
To run, untir'd, love's blessed race,
As meet for those, who face to face
  Over the grave their Lord have met.

CII.
CHURCHING OF WOMEN.

Is there, in bowers of endless spring,
    One known from all the seraph band
By softer voice, by smile and wing
    More exquisitely bland!
Here let him speed: to-day this hallow'd air
Is fragrant with a mother's first and fondest prayer.

Only let Heaven her fire impart,
    No richer incense breathes on earth:
" A spouse with all a daughter's heart,"
    Fresh from the perilous birth,
To the great Father lifts her pale glad eye,
Like a reviving flower when storms are hush'd on high.

O what a treasure of sweet thought
    Is here! what hope of joy and love

All in one tender bosom brought,
  For the all-gracious Dove
To brood o'er silently, and form for heaven
Each passionate wish and dream to dear affection given.

Her fluttering heart, too keenly blest,
  Would sicken, but she leans on Thee,
Sees Thee by faith on Mary's breast,
  And breathes serene and free.
Slight tremblings only of her veil declare *
Soft answers duly whisper'd to each soothing prayer.

We are too weak, when Thou dost bless,
  To bear the joy—help Virgin-born!
By thine own mother's first caress,
  That wak'd thy natal morn!
Help, by the unexpressive smile, that made
A heaven on earth around the couch where Thou wast laid!

---

* When the woman comes to this office, the rubric (as it was altered at the last review, directs that she be *decently apparelled*, i.e. as the custom and order was formerly, *with a white covering or veil*. Wheatley on the Common Prayer, c. xiii. sect. i. 3.

CIII.
COMMINATION.

THE prayers are o'er: why slumberest thou so long,
    Thou voice of sacred song?
Why swell'st thou not, like breeze from mountain cave,
    High o'er the echoing nave,
The white-rob'd priest, as otherwhile, to guide,
    Up to the altar's northern side?—
A mourner's tale of shame and sad decay
Keeps back our glorious sacrifice to-day:

The widow'd spouse of Christ: with ashes crown'd,
    Her Christmas robes unbound,
She lingers in the porch for grief and fear,
    Keeping her penance drear.—
O is it nought to you? that idly gay,
    Or coldly proud, ye turn away?
But if her warning tears in vain be spent,
Lo, to her alter'd eye the Law's stern fires are lent.

Commination.

Each awful curse, that on Mount Ebal rang,
    Peals with a direr clang
Out of that silver trump, whose tones of old
    Forgiveness only told.
And who can blame the mother's fond affright [b],
    Who sporting on some giddy height
Her infant sees, and springs with hurried hand
To snatch the rover from the dangerous strand?

But surer than all words the silent spell
    (So Grecian legends tell)
When to her bird, too early scap'd the nest,
    She bares her tender breast.
Smiling he turns and spreads his little wing,
    There to glide home, there safely cling.
So yearns our mother o'er each truant son,
So softly falls the lay in fear and wrath begun.

Wayward and spoil'd she knows ye: the keen blast
    That brac'd her youth, is past:
The rod of discipline, the robe of shame—
    She bears them in your name:

[b] Alluding to a beautiful anecdote in the Greek Anthology, tom. ii. 180. ed. Jacobs. See Pleasures of Memory, p. 133.

Only return and love. But ye perchance
    Are deeper plung'd in sorrow's trance:
Your God forgives, but ye no comfort take
Till ye have scourg'd the sins that in your conscience
    ache.

O heavy laden soul! kneel down and hear
    Thy penance in calm fear:
With thine own lips to sentence all thy sin;
    Then, by the judge within
Absolv'd, in thankful sacrifice to part
    For ever with thy sullen heart,
Nor on remorseful thoughts to brood, and stain
The glory of the Cross, forgiven and cheer'd in vain.

THE END.

www.ingramcontent.com/pod-product-compliance
Lightning Source LLC
Chambersburg PA
CBHW020858230426

43666CB00008B/1232